THE OXFORD ENGINEERING SCIENCE SERIES

General Editors

F. W. CRAWFORD, A. L. CULLEN, J. W. HUTCHINSON,
W. H. WITTRICK, L. C. WOODS

ECONOMICS
OF
ELECTRIC UTILITY
POWER GENERATION

W. D. MARSH

CLARENDON PRESS · OXFORD
OXFORD UNIVERSITY PRESS · NEW YORK
1980

Oxford University Press, Walton Street, Oxford OX2 6DP

OXFORD LONDON GLASGOW
NEW YORK TORONTO MELBOURNE WELLINGTON
IBADAN NAIROBI DAR ES SALAAM LUSAKA CAPE TOWN
KUALA LUMPUR SINGAPORE JAKARTA HONG KONG TOKYO
DELHI BOMBAY CALCUTTA MADRAS KARACHI

© Oxford University Press 1980

British Library Cataloguing in Publication Data

Marsh, W D
Economics of electric utility power generation.—
(Oxford engineering science series).
1. Electric utilities
I. Title II. Series
338.4'7'62131   HD9685.A2   80-40866
ISBN 0-19-856130-X

Printed in the United States of America

To Irene

Preface

THE TITLE may suggest that this book is a treatise on economics, but it was written out of the background and in the perspective of a power generation engineer, with the thought that it is better for an engineer to dabble in economics than for an economist to involve himself in engineering. There may be some disagreement on this point. But the intent is to provide a connection between the two disciplines that will be useful to those of varying academic backgrounds who find themselves involved in the energy field, particularly with respect to the generation of power by electric utility systems. To this end, the book devotes as much space to the engineering characteristics of generating units and generating systems as it does to the special economics and finance of utilities.

The book requires an understanding of algebra and basic physics. With instructional augmentation, it could form the basis of a graduate course in power-system engineering economics; or it could supplement such a course. For those outside the electric utility industry, or just entering it, the book may be a useful source book and reference.

The author wishes to express his appreciation to Dr. Charles Concordia, at whose suggestion this book was undertaken, and whose review of the typescript produced most valuable comments both as to organization and technical content. Others to whom the author is particularly indebted for their thoughtful contributions to the completeness and accuracy of the text include Dr. L. L. Garver, Messrs, G. J. Bonk, H. H. Heiges, R. W. Moisan, M. K. Morrison, and W. B. Wilson, of the General Electric Company, Dr. E. A. DeMeo of the Electric Power Research Institute, and Mr. J. A. Redman of the Central Electricity Generating Board of the United Kingdom.

Most sincere thanks are due to Miss Linda S. Christman for her diligence, competence, patience, and good humor while preparing the typescript and figures and in performing many valuable editorial tasks. The support of the management of the Electric Utility Systems Engineering Department of the General Electric Company in providing the opportunity and facilities for producing the work is gratefully acknowledged.

Schenectady, New York   W. D. M.
January 1980

Contents

List of Symbols

$A(y)$; a	Ad valorem taxes year y; level
$A_d(y)$; a_d	Accumulated depreciation year y; level
B	Debt ratio
b	Debt interest rate
C	Unit rating, power output
C_f; $C_f(y)$; $\bar{C}_f$	Capacity factor; year y; level
COE	Cost of electricity
CRF	Capital recovery factor
D	Plant cost, \$/kW
D_i	Incremental plant cost, \$/kW
$D(y)$; d	Depreciation for year y; level
$D_t(y)$; d_t	Tax depreciation year y; level
$D'(y)$; d'	Depreciation for normalizing year y; level
d/y	Days per year
DB	Declining-balance depreciation
DDB	Double declining-balance depreciation
DCF	Discounted cash flow
DCFR	Discounted cash flow return
E	Annual energy cost, \$/yr
E/C	Annual energy cost, \$/kW-yr
$E(y)$	General expense year y
e	Naperian constant, 2.71828 . . .
F; $F(y)$; $\bar{F}$	Fuel price, \$/GJ (\$/MBtu); for year y; level
f	Annual rate for declining-balance depreciation
FOH	Forced-outage hours
FCR(y); fcr	Fixed-charge rate year y; level

G	Annual capacity cost, \$/yr
G/C	Annual capacity cost, \$/kW-yr
g	Uniform gradient
H_1, H_2, etc.	Heat flow per unit time
h	Heat rate, kJ/kWh (Btu/kWh)
$I(y)$	Investment tax credit year y
$I_a(y)$; i_a	Amortization of investment tax credit, year y; level
$I_t(y)$	Taxable income year y
i	Minimum acceptable (overall) return on investment
j	Interest rate for sinking fund depreciation
K	Investment tax credit rate
K_d	D-factor
k	$(1 + u)/(1 + r)$
L	Load-carrying capacity (effective capacity)
LC	Lifecycle cost
LF_a	Annual load factor
LF_d	Daily load factor
LOLP	Loss-of-Load Probability
M	Slope characteristic of LOLP curve, MW
m	Tax depreciation life
MAR	Minimum acceptable return ($= i$)
N_h	Service hours per day
n	Book depreciation life, *and generally,* number of terms in a series
n_c	Length of amortization period for investment tax credit, years
n_1	Year of early retirement
O	Total operation and maintenance cost
O_f	Fixed operation and maintenance cost
O_v	Variable operation and maintenance cost
P	Present worth
P'	Investment
PL_a	Peak Load, annual
PL_d	Peak load, daily
PL_m	Peak load, monthly
PWF	Single payment present-worth factor
p_d	Daily probability of insufficient capacity
$Q(y)$	Conditional factor, deferred investment tax credit
q	Year before change to straight line in the declining-balance depreciation method

R	Uniform (level) annual payment
$R(y)$	Nonuniform payment year y
$R_1(y)$; r_1	Equity return, year y; level
$R_2(y)$; r_2	Interest on debt, year y; level
R_f	Forced-outage rate
R_y	Yearly reliability
r	Discount rate, interest rate
Rev (y)	Revenue year y
S	The amount at the end of a period or periods; future worth
S_c	System replacement capacity cost, \$/kW-yr
S_e	System replacement energy cost, \$/MWh
SH	Service hours
SL	Straight-line depreciation
SFF	Sinking-fund factor
SYD	Sum-of-years-digits depreciation
$T(y)$; $\overline{T}$	Income tax year y; level
$T_d(y)$	Deferred income tax year y
t	Statutory income tax rate
u	Inflation (escalation) rate
V_f	Value of fuel inventory
W	Energy, kWh/yr
$W(y)$	Conditional factor for amortization of investment tax credit
x	Characteristic exponent for D-factor
y	Year
$Z(y)$	Conditional factor for investment tax credit
η	Efficiency
λ	Incremental rate, \$/MWh

1
Introduction

The field of electric utility generation economics has developed over the past twenty-five years from the simple calculation of unit-generating cost in mills per kWh to the complex analysis of the operation and costs of complete systems of generating units. It is fundamental that this development has paralleled the development of improved methods for reliable and economic *operation* of power systems, because the function of economic analysis is to estimate 'how things will turn out'; and this requires that the economic analysis faithfully represent actual operations, technical as well as financial. For this reason, much of this book is devoted to an explanation of how generating units and systems of generating units operate, and how these operations affect the financial results of a utility organization. The following paragraphs outline this process with reference to the organization of the book.

PRINCIPLES OF ECONOMIC ANALYSIS

Economic analysis is the process by which the impact of a proposed action on the financial results of an organization's operations is measured. Its purpose is to supply one of the bases for management decision. The usual proposed action is one of capital investment in production facilities; and for an investor-owned company operating in a free economy, the impact to be measured is ordinarily that on net income, or profit. Thus, economic analysis methods, such as Payout Time, Discounted Cash Flow Return, and Net Present Worth, are commonly used in industry.

The economic and financial framework of electric utilities is different enough from that of other industries, however, to require a shift in the emphasis of economic analysis. Electric utilities fall into two categories: those which, although investor-owned, operate as regulated monopolies; and those which are owned by, or sponsored by, governments. In either case, there is external control of the return on investment and, accordingly, of the price of the product. As a result of these constraints, there has been a general adoption by electric utilities of the Revenue Requirements method of economic analysis because it fits the facts of the situation better. It begins with return on investment, then calculates the revenues required to achieve that return, the economic choice among alternatives being that which requires the smallest amount of revenue. This is the reverse of most of the previously cited methods, where revenues, or sales, are estimated and the alternative producing the highest return, or the shortest time for recovery of investment, is the choice. The difference is in point of view.

In Chapter 6 it is shown that the Discounted Cash Flow and Revenue Requirements methods produce identical results under equivalent assumptions. A fundamental reason for this is that they are both based on the financial and accounting facts of utility operations. This is essential, given the original definition of economic analysis: the methodology must simulate the profit and loss statement and the balance sheet. Because not all utilities are organized and financed in the same way, and because tax laws and accounting treatments vary, it is necessary to have an understanding of these matters, for they determine the parameters of economic analysis methodology. Chapters 2 and 3, 'Utility Organization' and 'Basic Accounting Principles,' attempt to provide this understanding.

The difference between accounting calculations and economic calculations is the recognition, in the latter, of the *time value of money*. Chapter 4 is a review of the principles governing this subject.

Economic Analysis Methods

Because the Revenue Requirements method is so widely used, it is given prime consideration in this book. The method is distinguished by its use of a *fixed-charge rate* by which the revenue requirement for capital is calculated. This, together with the costs of fuel, operating labor, and maintenance, becomes the total revenue requirement of a given investment in new generation. It is convenient and common, although somewhat imprecise, to refer to this total as 'cost of generation.' The fixed-charges portion is sometimes called 'cost of capital,' although this term is more frequently (and more accurately) used to denote the rate of return on invested capital.

The calculation of a fixed-charge rate may be quite complex, and in any event is variable, depending on the conditions of a specific utility. Chapter 5, 'Revenue Requirements: The Fixed-Charge Rate,' explains and derives formulas by which fixed-charge rates, both yearly and level, may be calculated for most conditions which may be encountered.

The use of the fixed-charge rate in Revenue Requirements analysis is explained in Chapter 6, 'Methods of Economic Analysis,' by means of simple examples. Other analysis methods are also discussed and compared.

REQUIREMENTS OF A GENERATION ECONOMIC STUDY

Like the legendary hero who 'leapt to his horse and galloped off in all directions,' it is tempting for the power engineer or economist to jump into his computer program and start calculating without adequate definition of the problem and its alternate solutions.

Comparability of Alternatives

The most important requirement of a generation economic study is that the alternate cases be determined to be truly comparable before their economic impacts are calculated. By 'comparable' is meant equal ability to serve a utility load with acceptable reliability.

The first step in fulfilling this requirement is to know something about the load to be served. The characteristics of utility loads and the parameters by which they are measured and described are discussed in Chapter 7, 'Electric Utility System Loads.'

The next step is to understand the operational requirements of generating units serving a load in time frames ranging from a few seconds to a few months. Chapter 8, 'System Operation,' discusses these requirements and the corresponding capabilities of common types of generating units. Also discussed in this chapter are the principles of economic commitment and dispatch, and the dispatch characteristics of generating units.

The final test of comparability is that alternate generation cases provide equal long-term reliability of the utility generation system. Alternate measures of system reliability are discussed, and a detailed description of the Loss-of-Load Probability method is included in Chapter 9, 'System Reliability: Reserves.'

Adequacy of Economic Data

A second general requirement of a generation economic study is that the data used be accurate and consistent. This requires an understanding and appreciation of the output and efficiency of thermodynamic cycles, the nature of fuels and their heating values, the characteristics of operation and maintenance costs, the constituents of capital cost, and the effects of inflation and interest during construction. These subjects are discussed in Chapter 10, 'Economic Characteristics of Generating Units,' with respect to coal-, oil-, and gas-fired steam units, gas turbines, combined (topping) cycles, and nuclear units.

PROCEDURES OF GENERATION ECONOMIC STUDIES

Given alternate generation plans, an economic analysis methodology, and adequate data, it now becomes necessary to devise a study procedure that will ensure comparability of cases and produce valid economic measurements. The next four chapters discuss the two major categories of study procedure: total system analysis, and direct unit comparison.

Total System Analysis

The economic analysis method (whether Revenue Requirements or another) requires inputs: capital (investment) costs and annual production costs (fuel, operation, and maintenance). The purpose of total system cost analysis is to develop these inputs in such a way that comparability of cases is assured. The process is one of system reliability analysis to determine required timing of capital investment in new generation, and detailed simulation of system operation to calculate annual production costs.

Thus, there are two levels of simulation involved in the total-generation economic study: first, that of the economic methodology, which, given investments and annual production expenses, simulates the impact on the financial results of the profit and loss, or income, statement; and second, that which simulates system operation in order to obtain realistic production-cost inputs for the economic analysis.

The total system study is distinguished by its cognizance of all system generating units and their effects on the economics of alternate proposed units, and by the length of the study period—usually fifteen to twenty years. A study period of this length requires estimates of data for the future—loads, costs, etc.—but this does not mean that the study constitutes a prediction of the future, even though its results, arrayed in year-by-year splendor, may have that appearance. The objective is always merely to provide the economic basis for a current business decision. Economic results are, of course, influenced by the projection of future conditions, and it is frequently necessary to vary future study parameters to appraise that influence in the face of uncertainty.

Total system analysis procedures are not practicable without the aid of computer programs for reliability calculations and production-cost simulation, and most utility organizations have, or have access to, programs which are adequate for the purpose. Functional descriptions of such programs and their use in total system analysis are given in Chapter 11, 'Total System Analysis,' together with discussions of alternate approaches, including financial simulation. References are given to detailed descriptions of computer programs.

In order to assist the reader in applying the procedures of total system analysis, Chapter 12, 'Problems in Total System Analysis,' discusses several common generation economic problems, including choice of unit type, unit size, and the influence of transmission. Chapter 13, 'Analysis of Storage and Renewable Energy Sources,' is devoted to the special considerations of such devices as pumped-storage hydro, storage batteries, and solar and wind power conversion.

Direct Unit Comparisons

In a sense, the total system analysis is easier to carry off with impunity than direct unit comparison, because the reliability calculations and production-cost simulation of the former tend to force comparability of cases. As described in Chapter 14, direct unit comparisons calculate the generation costs of only the units under consideration; any differences in their impacts on system reliability and operation must be adjusted for by the analyst, based on an understanding of system reliability and economic operation. Direct unit comparisons are appropriate only under certain specified circumstances.

The methods of Cost of Electricity ($/MWh), Lifecycle Costs, and Screening Curves are all defined and illustrated with examples.

SUMMARY AND FUTURE DEVELOPMENT

In the final chapter, the field of generation economics is considered in retrospect and in prospect. The developing areas of inflation, environmental impacts, and the treatment of uncertainty are discussed, and the fundamental viability of economic studies reasserted. It is noted that a utility manager, in considering a decision with respect to generation capacity, must assess many factors, political and societal as well as economic and financial. Although he may be able to identify the one 'economic choice,' his decision may very well be otherwise, as he balances all factors against the varied objectives of his organization. This fact does not diminish the value or importance of economic and financial studies, if for no other reason than that they provide indispensable measures of the cost of concession to other, noneconomic factors. It is always important to know what *should* be done, even though it may be, pragmatically, impossible.

TERMINOLOGY—COSTS

Although most of the terminology used in the book is believed to be common to English-speaking countries, there are undoubtedly some exceptions. Where these are known to the author, the text recognizes the alternate terminology; where not, it is hoped that the Glossary will bridge the gap, in addition to providing clarification for readers of varying backgrounds of knowledge.

The 'per unit' (p.u.) system of the electrical engineering field has been adopted, where appropriate, for calculations. The value of a quantity expressed in per unit is one one-hundredth of its value expressed in percent. The SI prefixes k (10^3) and M (10^6) have been used, for convenience, with non-SI units such as $ and Btu.

The dollar has been used as the monetary unit, and where absolute costs were required, a level estimated to be appropriate to the mid-1980s has been used. This cost level, however, is critical to neither economic principles nor the results of study examples.

In the business of *forecasting* the prices of things, it is necessary to distinguish between price changes that result from such technical factors as commodity shortages, sometimes called 'escalation,' and changes due to monetary inflation, sometimes called 'inflation of the economy.' But in *economic studies*, the results of price forecasts are used only as inputs, and the distinction is unnecessary. Some economic studies have omitted monetary inflation on the basis that it affects all alternatives alike, but this is simply not true. Consequently, it is recommended that the costs used for any time period be the best estimates based on the compound effects of both technical changes and monetary inflation; hence there is no need to distinguish between the terms 'escalation' and 'inflation,' and both are used in this book to express total price change.

2
Utility Organization

A utility organization operates for the purpose of providing high-quality electric service to the designated service area. In doing this it invests borrowed capital, consumes labor and materials, and charges a price for its product which is the sum of its costs, including return to investors. In these operations its objective is to produce electricity at the lowest possible cost to the user. One may question the validity of this statement of objective, especially with reference to investor-owned utilities operating in a free-market economy, where the objective of economic enterprises is commonly considered to be the maximization of return to the owners. The question may seem especially pertinent considering that nearly all electric utilities are legal monopolies operating without competition. The countervailing factor, however, is that utilities are also nearly always subject to government regulation, usually on the basis of allowing revenues sufficient to produce a 'fair return' on the invested capital.

In this function, the allowed return is usually expressed as an overall percentage of a defined 'rate base' which, in general, consists of the net, or depreciated, value of original plant investment. In some cases, an allowance may be made for the higher costs of replacement of plant. To this allowed return are added the necessary expenses of fuel, operation, and maintenance to arrive at allowable total revenue, which is expressed in terms of 'rates'* (prices of electricity in $/kW and/or $/MWh) to be charged consumers. Because changes (usually increases) in permitted electricity rates require formal requests with lengthy documentation and public hearings, some regulatory authorities permit immediate, automatic 'pass-through' of fuel-cost increases to the rate structure to be confirmed by subsequent hearings.

These provisions would appear to limit the incentives of utility management, but government regulation, in addition to ensuring an adequate yet not excessive return, has the corollary function of encouraging efficient operation for the

---

* Not to be confused with 'taxes,' the meaning of the term in British usage.

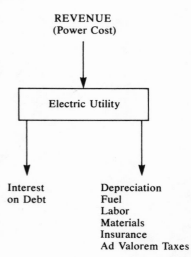

Fig. 2.1. Money flow in a government-owned utility.

benefit of consumers; and the direct and obvious measure of this is the magnitude of the electric revenues required to support an adequate return. Utility management, therefore, must have as its objective the lowest possible price of electricity, and in economic analysis this is the fundamental criterion. In those situations where electric energy competes directly with other forms of energy, the need for a criterion of lowest cost is even more apparent.

GOVERNMENT–OWNED UTILITIES

There are two broad categories of utility organizations that require consideration: government-owned utilities, and investor-owned utilities. Figure 2.1 shows, for a government-owned utility, the flow of money from electric revenues into an electric utility and the flow of money out in the form of interest on debt and expenses for the production of electricity. Debt represents money borrowed for a specified period of time at a fixed rate of interest. Long-term debt is incurred for the financing of fixed assets, such as generation plant, and its term is comparable to the life of the assets, e.g., thirty years. It may be repaid in installments or at the end of the borrowing term, at which time the debt is said to be 'retired.' Short-term, or temporary, debt comprises funds borrowed for a period of a year or less for the purpose of financing operations, i.e. working capital. Its source is usually the banking industry.

The sources of long-term debt of government-owned utilities are variable. In some cases, the utility may sell bonds directly to the public at interest rates determined by the open securities market. Or, the owning governmental body may itself issue bonds to the public, pledging the revenues of the utility as security, in which case the bonds may be termed 'revenue bonds.' Another very common procedure is for the government to make direct loans to the utility under conditions of term and interest rate consistent with those existing in the free bond market for similar securities. Whatever the financing arrangement, the result is to impose upon the managers of the government-owned utility financial discipline and measurement similar to those of investor-owned organizations.

The interest on debt is one component of the power cost, or required revenue. Suppliers of capital require more than interest, however; they require that their investment be recovered when the bonds mature, and for this purpose the utility must set aside money from its revenues to accumulate the recovery of investment during the life of the indebtedness. Another way of thinking of this accumulation of funds is to consider it a reserve to allow the replacement of the equipment for which the debt was incurred when the equipment becomes obsolete or unusable. In this sense it is called *depreciation,* and so in principle the same accumulation performs two purposes: (1) it provides money for retiring the debt at maturity, and (2) it provides funds to replace equipment that is no longer serviceable. Obviously the same money cannot be used twice; but if it is used to retire debt, then the same or other investors will be willing to provide new funds to replace the equipment, and both objectives will have been accomplished.

There are now two annual costs that have been identified: (1) interest, or return *on* the investment, and (2) recovery *of* the investment, or depreciation. Other annual expenses required to operate the utility are fuel, labor, materials, and the usual insurance to protect against catastrophic breakdown of equipment and damage to the property or person of others.

A final category of expense is taxes. A utility owned by a government will ordinarily be exempt from income, or profit, taxes. It may, nevertheless, be allowed to charge rates for electricity that will permit a profit, or excess of revenues over the costs of interest and operating expenses. Such profit is not usually returned to the owning government, but is held as a reserve against the possibility of future operating losses and to provide an internal source of capital funds for investment in future facilities. Such a utility may not, however, be exempt from property (ad valorem) taxes levied by the local governments in whose territories it owns properties.

INVESTOR–OWNED UTILITIES

In Fig. 2.2 a diagram of money flow is shown for an investor-owned utility. The items for depreciation, fuel, labor, materials, ad valorem taxes, and insurance expenses are identical to those of Fig. 2.1. The differences are in the addition of income taxes as expense and of shareholders as investors. In investor-owned utilities the funds for capital investment are provided publicly by bondholders ('debt capital') and by shareholders ('equity capital'), usually in about equal proportions. Bonds are either unsecured ('debentures') or secured by a mortgage on the assets of the utility.

The shareholders who provide the balance of the capital require a higher rate of return than do bondholders, because of the higher risk involved in what

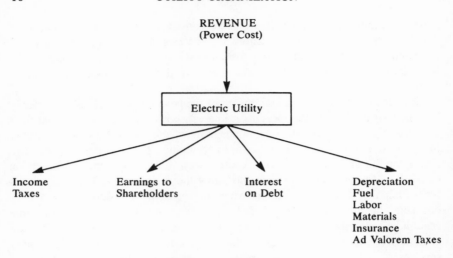

Fig. 2.2. Money flow in an investor-owned utility.

amounts to an unsecured investment with less assurance of return. The most prevalent types of shares are *preferred* and *common*. The preferred shares of stock have first claim on the earnings of the utility and pay a fixed return expressed either in absolute monetary value per share or as a percentage of an arbitrary 'par' value. Most preferred-stock issues do not carry voting rights and hence do not reflect control over the company, but only ownership.

Common shares, on the other hand, represent voting rights and control and are entitled to all of the residual earnings after the bond interest and the preferred dividends have been paid. Earnings attributable to all shareholders are also considered as taxable income to the utility. Hence the utility's net earnings are reckoned after income taxes. These earnings are not all returned to the shareholders in the form of dividends. A portion, typically 30% to 40%, is retained in much the same way as the profits of a government-owned utility, to provide capital funds for expansion, and as a reserve against years of low profits.

It is important to note that these retained earnings, together with funds withheld for depreciation and tax accruals, may, in either an investor- or a government-owned utility, provide significantly more than half of the capital funds required for expansion of facilities.

COMPARISON OF UTILITY OWNERSHIP

It is apparent in comparing Figs. 2.1 and 2.2 that the total cost of producing electricity in an investor-owned utility is greater than with government ownership because of income taxes and the higher cost of equity capital. It may be argued, however, that regardless of the kind of utility ownership, the *total* cost to society of taxes and electric power is about the same. Figure 2.3 is a simple diagram

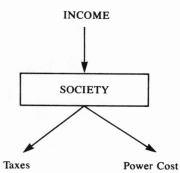

Fig. 2.3. Cost to society.

showing income to society, either gross national product or some other measure of income, and the outlay that society makes for power cost and for taxes to support government. If the electric power system is investor-owned, then the amount of taxes that must be paid directly by society will be lower and the power cost higher than under government ownership. There is thus, in principle, no particular choice of good or bad as far as economics is concerned, but only a matter of preference in the way of collecting taxes and paying power bills. Furthermore, and this is the major thrust of the discussion to this point, the measure of the economic efficiency or effectiveness of an electric utility is its ability to produce electricity at minimum cost, or minimum required revenue, whatever the economic framework within which it operates.

3
Basic Accounting Principles

The basic purpose of a corporate accounting system is to record, or account for, (1) the ownership of the corporation; (2) the funds, or cash, and the physical property belonging to the corporation; and (3) the operating results, or profit and loss, of the corporation. In the cash-based system, which is the simplest, two kinds of accounts are used: *capital* (sometimes called 'real') and *operating* (sometimes called 'nominal'). The capital accounts are further divided into *asset* and *liability* accounts; the operating, into *income* and *expense* accounts.

Accounting systems are 'double-entry'; i.e. each account is conceived as having two columns, the left one called *debit* or *debtor,* and the right one always called *credit*. The origin of these terms is in thirteenth-century Roman commercial practice, where double-entry bookkeeping was first used only for customer (debtor) accounts (*debet* = 'he owes') and vendor (creditor) accounts (*credit* = 'he trusts'). In modern accounting, the terms have lost these intrinsic meanings and are descriptive of little more than 'left' and 'right,' respectively. They are used as nouns, adjectives, and verbs.

CASH–BASED ACCOUNTING

In order to explain some of these accounting ideas, a simple cash-based accounting system, such as would actually be used only in a small club or other informal association, will be described first.

Capital Transactions

A cash-based accounting system would begin with the sale of capital stock. The double entries in the capital accounts are:

Capital Stock		Cash	
	300	300	

The purchase of a production plant produces:

Cash		Plant		Capital Stock	
300	300	300			300

Cash and *Plant* are asset accounts. The established convention is that when asset accounts have a positive balance, it is shown on the debit side. Liability accounts, such as *Capital Stock,* carry the positive balance on the credit side. Note that when the cash balance was reduced to zero in the purchase of the production plant, an entry was made on the credit side rather than subtracting from the debit side. This reflects the double-entry principle: there are always two entries for any transaction or event, one a debit, and one a credit. Which entry produces an increase and which a decrease depends on the kind of account: asset or liability.

The status of all of the capital accounts at any time is reported on a *Balance Sheet:*

Beginning Balance Sheet

Assets		Liabilities and Capital	
Cash	0	Capital Stock	300
Plant	300		

The left-right orientation, corresponding to that of positive balances in capital accounts, is traditional but not universal. The annual reports of some utilities list the balance sheet vertically, usually showing assets first.

Operating Transactions

Capital accounts are continuous—they reflect the existence of corporate obligations or financial values. Hence they endure for the life of the obligations or of the corporation itself. Operating accounts, in contrast, endure only until the end of the period for which the operations of the corporation are being reported. Then they are 'closed,' or reduced to zero, ready to record the next period's operations.

A cash-based system would record revenues as follows:

Revenues		Cash	
	100	100	

Expense is recorded:

Labor		Materials		Insurance		Cash	
40		40		6		100	40
							40
							6

Revenues is an income account, while *Labor, Materials,* and *Insurance* are expense accounts. Income accounts carry a positive balance on the credit side, expense accounts on the debit side. This is necessary, given the convention of positive balances described above for the asset and liability accounts.

At the end of the accounting period, the operating accounts are closed to a summarization account, *Profit and Loss:*

Revenues		Labor		Materials		Insurance	
100	100	40	40	40	40	6	6

Profit and Loss	
40	100
40	
6	

The Profit and Loss account shows a credit (profit) balance of 14. At this point, a decision is made to pay 8 of the profit to the stockholders in the form of dividends:

Cash		Profit and Loss	
100	40	40	100
	40	40	
	6	6	
	8	8	

The remainder of the profit is closed to a new capital account, *Retained Earnings:*

Profit and Loss		Retained Earnings	
40	100		6
40			
6			
8			
6			

The Retained Earnings account is sometimes called *Surplus* or *Earned Surplus.* In all of these transactions, note the double entries, debit and credit.

Ending Statements

The balance sheet at the end of the accounting period is the status, or balance, of all the capital accounts.

Ending Balance Sheet

Assets		Liabilities	
Cash	6	Capital Stock	300
Plant	300	Retained Earnings	6
	306		306

The *operating statement,* sometimes called income statement, or profit and loss statement, reports the process by which the operating profit or loss was realized. The terms 'profit' and 'net income' are interchangeable.

Operating Statement

Revenues		100
Expense		
Labor	40	
Materials	40	
Insurance	6	86
Net Income		14

Note that in this cash-based accounting system, the net income, less dividends, is exactly equal to the increase in cash between the beginning and ending balance sheets.

ACCRUAL ACCOUNTING

In cash-based accounting, all transactions (not including the closing entries) involve cash receipts or disbursements. Because of time-lags in collecting and disbursing cash, this usually misstates the operating results. For example, at the end of an accounting period, there will be product that has been delivered, and corresponding revenues billed, for which no cash yet has been received. In accrual accounting, this is recorded by an asset account called *Accounts Receivable,* which substitutes for the cash account:

Revenues Billed		Accounts Receivable	
	100	100	

When some of the revenue billings are paid, the transaction is:

Accounts Receivable		Cash	
100	50	50	

Similarly, when materials are purchased they are not paid for immediately. Furthermore, even though received, the materials may not be used in production immediately. These two time-lags are handled thus:

Materials Inventory		Materials Expense		Accounts Payable	
20		20			40

Here, half of the materials go into production during the accounting period as expense, and half are retained in the asset account, *Materials Inventory,* for future production. When some of the bills are paid, the entry is:

Cash		Accounts Payable	
50	20	20	40

Insurance premiums are frequently paid in advance; hence only a portion should be charged to the current accounting period. As before, a new asset account (*Prepaid Insurance*) is set up to record this deferred expense:

Cash		Insurance Expense		Prepaid Insurance	
50	20	2		4	
	6				

The labor expense of 40 has not yet been paid, and since there is only 24 in the cash account, it will be necessary to take a short-term loan,

Cash		Short-Term Loans	
50	20		30
30	6		

which will permit paying the labor force:

Cash		Labor Expense	
50	20	40	
30	6		
	40		

There is, however, interest on the loan that must be paid:

Cash		Interest Expense	
50	20	3	
30	6		
	40		
	3		

Although not the case in the past, *depreciation* is now universally regarded as a valid and necessary expense. It has only a remote relationship to a cash expenditure, that being the end-of-life replacement of production plant. For utility plants, depreciation expense is usually in the range from 2.5% to 3.5% per year. Since there is no actual cash expense payment, the offsetting credit is to a new capital account, *Accumulated Depreciation,* sometimes called depreciation reserve:

Depreciation Expense		Accumulated Depreciation	
10			10

Ending Statements

Operating Statement

Revenues		100
Expense		
Materials	20	
Insurance	2	
Labor	40	
Interest	3	
Depreciation	10	75
Net Income		25

Of this net income, 5 is paid out in dividends, resulting in a credit to cash, and the transfer of only 20 to retained earnings.

Ending Balance Sheet

Assets		Liabilities	
Cash	6	Capital Stock	300
Plant	300	Retained Earnings	20
Accounts Receivable	50	Accounts Payable	20
Materials Inventory	20	Short-Term Loans	30
Prepaid Insurance	4	Accumulated Depreciation	10
	380		380

The accumulated depreciation is frequently shown on the asset side as a subtractor from the plant account, yielding *Net Plant*. Prepaid Insurance may be aggregated with other similar accounts and shown on the balance sheet as *Deferred Debits*. Similarly, *Deferred Credits*, on the liability side, may be used to describe such situations as an expense which is properly chargeable to the currrent accounting period, but for which payment is not due until some future time. The double-entries for such an item would have been a debit to some expense account and a credit to *Accrued Expense*, the former reflected in the income statement and the latter in the balance sheet as a constituent of deferred credits.

Cash Reconciliation

Working Capital is a term applied to the cash tied up in short-term assets and liabilities needed in the day-to-day operation of the business. In this example it consists of Accounts Receivable plus Materials Inventory plus Prepaid Insurance minus Accounts Payable, which equals 54. Because in our example all these accounts began the period at zero balance, the increase in working capital is also 54.

Since in accrual accounting there is no obvious relationship between the increase in cash and net income, a cash report, or statement of *Source and Disposition of Funds,* is required:

Source and Disposition of Funds

Cash at beginning of period		0
Net Income	25	
Depreciation	10	
Cash from Operations		35
Sale of Capital Stock	300	
Short-Term Loans	30	
Cash from External Sources		330
Total Funds Available		365
Disposition of Funds:		
Construction Expenditure		300
Dividends Paid		5
Net Increase in Working Capital		54
Total Funds Dispersed		359
Cash at End of Period		6
		365

From this statement, one can see why the increase in cash is not equal to the net income. The cash from sale of capital stock is just balanced by construction expenditures, so in this case these transactions may be ignored. The net income would have been equal to the cash increase except that: (1) depreciation expense, which was deducted from revenues in arriving at net income, did not involve a cash outlay, so it must be added back in; (2) there were revenues that were not cash (Accounts Receivable), expenses that were not cash (Accounts Payable), and expenses not rightly chargeable to this accounting period (Prepaid Insurance, Materials Inventory), all of which reflect an investment of cash in working capital; (3) cash dividends were paid out of net income; and, (4) of course, the short-term loan represents external cash that has nothing whatever to do with net income. If this enterprise were to liquidate its working capital, it would have enough funds (54 + 6 = 60) to pay off the short-term loan and have 30 left over, which is just the amount generated from operations less the dividend payment.

The cash generated from operations, sometimes called *internal funds* or *cash flow,* is a figure of merit almost as important as net income. This is particularly so in the utility industry, where the need for funds for plant expansion is so great. The more of these funds that can be generated internally and reinvested in new plant, the less is the need for external financing with its higher cost and its potential for diluting the equity of existing shareholders.

DEPRECIATION

Depreciation is the accounting process by which the initial investment in a physical asset is distributed over the expected life of the asset in some systematic, rational method, as an annual cost of operation of the enterprise. (Actually, it is the initial investment less estimated salvage value at time of retirement that is depreciated; but this produces only a change in the base to which depreciation calculations are applied, and hence will be considered understood without further reference in the discussions to follow.) The use of depreciation is in response to the needs of the corporation, as a 'legal person,' to avoid wasting its assets so that it may continue in business indefinitely. It is also in response to the requirement of investors that their investments be preserved. In this latter respect, but only indirectly related to the subject of depreciation, is the not infrequent practice of requiring that the corporation establish a sinking fund for the retirement of bonds. This is a real fund, separate from the funds of the corporation, into which is paid an annuity such that, with interest, the fund will amount to the face value of the bonds at the end of their term.

Sinking-Fund Method

This practice, no doubt, inspired the method of depreciation called *sinking-fund depreciation*. It is used without regard to whether the corporation has or has not bonded indebtedness requiring real sinking funds. It is merely a systematic, rational method of determining the annual charge for depreciation. It is based on a fictitious sinking fund, presumed to be set up to recover the initial investment at interest rate, j over the life of the asset, n. The depreciation charge each year is the level sinking-fund annuity *plus* the interest on the accumulated depreciation. The level sinking-fund annuity is the initial investment times the sinking-fund factor (SFF), which may be found in standard interest tables or calculated as

$$\text{SFF} = \frac{j}{(1 + j)^n - 1}. \qquad (3.1)$$

For example, with an initial investment of 1, an interest rate $j = 0.12$, and a life $n = 5$ years, the depreciation charges $D(y)$, paid at the end of year y, and accumulated depreciation $A_d(y)$, at the end of year y, are:

$D(1) = 1 \times 0.15741 = 0.15741 \ (= \text{SFF}).$
$A_d(1) = 0.15741.$
$D(2) = 0.15741 + (0.12 \times 0.15741) = 0.17630.$
$A_d(2) = 0.15741 + 0.17630 = 0.33371.$
$D(3) = 0.15741 + (0.12 \times 0.33371) = 0.19745.$
$A_d(3) = 0.33371 + 0.19745 = 0.53116.$
$D(4) = 0.15741 + (0.12 \times 0.53116) = 0.22115.$
$A_d(4) = 0.53116 + 0.22115 = 0.75231.$
$D(5) = 0.15741 + (0.12 \times 0.75231) = 0.24769.$
$A_d(5) = 0.75231 + 0.24769 = 1.00000.$

In general, then,

$$D(y) = \text{SFF}(1 + j)^{y-1}, \tag{3.2}$$

and

$$A_d(y) = \text{SFF}[(1 + j)^y - 1]/j. \tag{3.3}$$

As stated earlier, this process of building up a sinking fund is purely fictitious—a mechanism for establishing a sequence of annual depreciation charges. The calculation of interest on the accumulated depreciation had no financial impli-

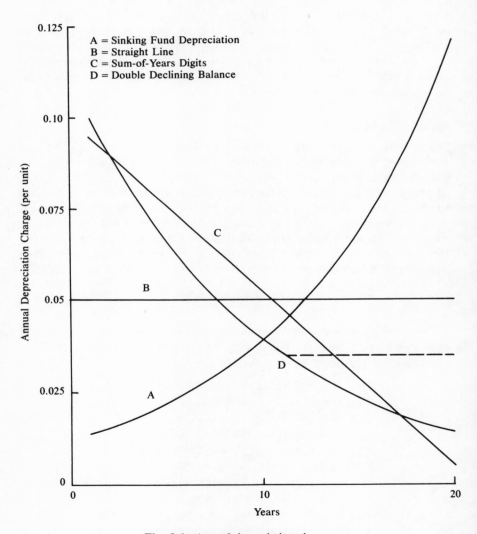

Fig. 3.1. Annual depreciation charge.

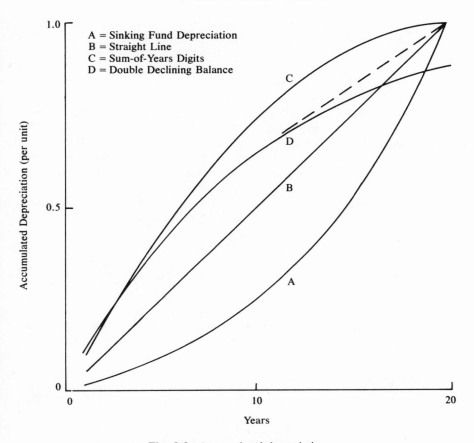

Fig. 3.2. Accumulated depreciation.

cations whatsoever. Curve A of Fig. 3.1 shows the annual depreciation charge for a 20-year depreciation life. Curve A of Fig. 3.2 shows the accumulated depreciation.

Straight-Line Depreciation

A simpler and more common method of depreciation is called *straight-line depreciation* (SL). Here the annual depreciation charge represents an equal allocation of initial investment over the depreciation life. Again taking the initial investment to be unity,

$$D(y) = \frac{1}{n};\tag{3.4}$$

$$A_d(y) = \frac{y}{n}.\tag{3.5}$$

In Fig. 3.1 and 3.2, Curve B gives annual depreciation charges and accumulated depreciation, respectively, for the straight-line method.

Sum-of-Years Digits

Sinking-fund depreciation is 'slow' relative to straight-line; i.e. the depreciation accumulates less rapidly in the early years of life. In contrast are two methods of 'fast' depreciation. The first is called *sum-of-years digits* (SYD). In this method, the annual charge is a fraction of initial investment whose numerator is the remaining life and whose denominator is the sum-of-the-years digits:

$$D(y) = \frac{n - y + 1}{(1 + 2 + 3 + \cdots + n)} = \frac{n - y + 1}{\dfrac{n(n + 1)}{2}} ; \qquad (3.6)$$

$$A_d(y) = 1 - \frac{\dfrac{(n - y)(n - y + 1)}{2}}{\dfrac{n(n + 1)}{2}} = 1 - \frac{(n - y)(n - y + 1)}{n(n + 1)}. \qquad (3.7)$$

In Figs. 3.1 and 3.2, Curve C gives annual depreciation charges and accumulated depreciation for the SYD method.

Declining-Balance Method

The second fast depreciation method is *declining-balance depreciation* (DB). Here, a fixed rate is applied not to the initial investment but to the balance of the investment after the depreciation charges of prior years have been subtracted. In the United States, federal income tax regulations permit a maximum rate equal to twice the straight-line rate; hence it is there commonly called *double declining balance* (DDB). If the annual rate is f,

$$
\begin{aligned}
D(1) &= f. \\
D(2) &= f(1 - f), \\
D(3) &= f\{1 - [f + f(1 - f)]\} \\
&= f(1 - f)^2, \\
D(y) &= f(1 - f)^{y-1},
\end{aligned} \qquad (3.8)
$$

and,

$$A_d(y) = f[1 + (1 - f) + (1 - f)^2 + \cdots (1 - f)^{y-1}]. \qquad (3.9)$$

Multiplying by $(1 - f)$:

$$(1 - f)A_d(y) = f[1 - f + (1 - f)^2 + \cdots (1 - f)^y]. \qquad (3.10)$$

Substracting eqn (3.9) from eqn (3.10):

$$A_d(y) = 1 - (1 - f)^y. \qquad (3.11)$$

The value of $A_d(y)$ approaches 1.0 only as y approaches infinity. The solid part of curve D of Fig. 3.2 shows that, for a 20-year life, the accumulated depreciation is only about 88% of initial investment if f is double the straight-line rate ($f = 2 \times 1/20$). Consequently, the usual practice is to switch to straight-line depreciation after some particular year. The dashed curves of Figs. 3.1 and 3.2 show this switch in the year in which the straight-line depreciation on the remaining balance is just equal to the declining-balance depreciation.

As can be imagined, combinations of these four depreciation methods have been developed and are sometimes used. Fast methods such as SYD and DB are almost universally used for tax purposes. Practice is divided among straight-line and fast methods for purposes of reporting net income to stockholders. The sinking-fund method is rarely used today for any purpose.

Depreciation Life

Unlike the situation with the many small items, such as distribution poles, insulators, and fuses, that are used in great quantities in utility plants, the expected life of a generating unit cannot routinely be determined by statistical analysis of historical mortality. The retirement of a generating unit is apt to be determined more by economic obsolescence than by wear-out, and this must be taken into account in making life estimates for depreciation purposes. When a unit is retired before the end of its originally estimated life, there will be an undepreciated balance which must be debited to depreciation expense and credited to accumulated depreciation. If the balance is not too large, and depending on the rules of taxing and regulatory bodies, these charges may be made in the year of retirement; otherwise, they may be spread out (amortized) over an arbitrary future period of years. This is to avoid an excessive perturbation in taxes and earnings in a single year. In either case, the initial cost of the unit is ultimately removed from the Plant account with a credit entry, and from the Accumulated Depreciation account with a debit entry.

When a generating unit remains in service after the end of its depreciation life, further depreciation charges stop. But the unit initial cost remains in both the Plant and Accumulated Depreciation accounts until actual retirement occurs.

This depreciation process differs from that used for the numerous small items mentioned above, which are ordinarily treated as homogeneous groups. Average group lives are determined as a basis for establishing annual depreciation charges which are used without continuous adjustment for early or late actual retirements: it is expected that this retirement dispersion will even out over a large number of items over a long period of time. Periodically, analyses are made to adjust depreciation lives to accord with experience. But this group-basis depreciation accounting is not often used for generation plant.

Choice of Depreciation Method

Many arguments can be advanced in favor of using fast, slow, or specific depreciation methods in accounting for net income to shareholders. A consideration in the view of regulatory bodies is whether the method treats fairly the current, as opposed to future, power users. This question arises because electricity rates are most frequently based on allowing the utility to earn a specified return (which comprises interest paid to bondholders and net income attributable to shareholders) on invested capital. A fast depreciation method, for example, tends to produce a lower net income in early years, which means that, for the same return on invested capital, the utility must receive relatively higher revenues in the early years. The reverse is true in later years. This implies higher electricity rates for current customers than for future customers.

Some utility managers might favor a fast method to increase cash flow, or might espouse a slow method for conservatism or to more nearly match the loss of life of equipment. But the most common practice is to use the straight-line method. Its charm is in its simplicity and linearity.

As explained below, depreciation for income tax purposes is most often one of the fast methods.

TAX ACCOUNTING

The three most common kinds of taxes levied on utilities are ad valorem, or property taxes; gross income, or revenue taxes; and profit, or (net) income taxes. The first two are usually specified percentages of their bases, hence involve no particular complications. Income taxes, however, may be very complex, largely because they may be levied by national taxing authorities to achieve economic or social goals in addition to the mere production of government revenue.

Taxable Income

Income tax is calculated as a statutory rate applied to a taxable income which is rarely the same as the net income reported to shareholders (commonly called 'book income') and used by regulatory bodies to determine return on investment. The significant difference is that the depreciation lives and methods permitted and used for calculating taxable income are not the same as those permitted or required for book income. The resulting complications make it quite necessary and proper for a corporation to keep two sets of accounts: one for taxes, and one for 'books.'

It is advantageous for a utility to use a fast, or accelerated, depreciation method, such as SYD or DB, for taxes, not because it reduces the total income tax to be paid, but because it defers the payment of taxes. This effectively increases cash flow, which in turn defers the need for new external financing with its associated interest costs. If, further, the tax depreciation life can be shorter than the expected physical life, this produces additional desirable cash flow.

The process by which fast depreciation defers but does not ultimately reduce taxes may be seen from Fig. 3.1 by comparing SYD with straight-line depreciation. The higher depreciation in the early years of life, which produces lower taxable income, is exactly offset by relatively lower depreciation, hence higher taxable income, in later years. This is true no matter which two methods are compared because total depreciation equals initial investment in all methods, including those which use a short depreciation life for tax purposes.

Normalized Accounting

In the same way that choice of book depreciation method can affect the magnitude of current versus future earnings levels, so can the choice of tax depreciation methods, by influencing current versus future income tax expense. Here the concern is that fast tax depreciation understates current taxes, hence overstates current earnings, thus permitting lower current revenues or power rates—all at the expense of users who come later. This refreshing advocacy of the welfare of future generations finds expression in a 'have-your-cake-and-eat-it' accounting procedure known as *normalizing*.

In this process, fast depreciation is used in calculating income taxes actually to be paid. But the income statement for shareholders is prepared as though the straight-line or another 'normal' depreciation method had been used for calculating taxes. Thus, in the early years, the tax expense shown on the income statement is larger than the tax actually paid to the taxing authority. In later years, the reverse is true, and the desired avoidance of swings in earnings and electricity rates is achieved, while also obtaining the cash-flow benefit of fast tax depreciation.

The following two statements will illustrate the accounting procedure.

Income Tax Statement

Revenues		100
Operating Expenses	41	
Depreciation	16	
Interest on Debt	15	
Total Deductions		72
Taxable Income		28
Tax at 50%		14

Operating Statement

Revenues		100
Operating Expenses	41	
Depreciation	10	
Income Taxes	14	
Deferred Income Taxes	3	
Interest on Debt	15	
Total Expense		83
Net Income		17

These statements are for an early year in the life of the plant, when tax depreciation is greater than book depreciation (16 vs. 10). The deferred tax is the difference between the tax that would have been calculated, had the book depreciation been used in the income tax statement, and the actual tax. It is, of course, the product of the tax rate and the difference in book and tax depreciation amounts, or 0.5(16 − 10). In later years, the deferred tax becomes negative because tax depreciation is less than book depreciation.

Since the deferred tax is an expense debit for which there is no offsetting cash credit entry, a new capital account, *Accumulated Deferred Income Tax,* is created, which appears on the liability side of the balance sheet to accept the credit entry. The credit balance in this account will increase during the life of the plant until the tax depreciation becomes less than the book depreciation. At this point, the deferred tax on the income statement becomes a negative expense (credit) and the offsetting debit to the Accumulated Deferred Income Tax account begins to reduce its balance until it reaches zero at end of life. This is true for a single asset; but in a growing utility, the negative values rarely appear on the financial statements because the bulk of the assets are in the first half of life.

Flow-Through Accounting

The normalization procedure is not always used with fast tax depreciation. The alternative is simply to show on the income statement the taxes as actually incurred and paid. The imaginary early-year tax savings and late-year tax losses (relative to normal straight-line depreciation) are said to 'flow through' to net income, and hence the name.

Investment Tax Credit

Part of the philosophy of fast tax depreciation is the idea that, by increasing cash flow, it encourages investment in new facilities, a frequent objective of national tax policy. Even more encouraging is another device, the investment tax credit, which allows an actual, direct reduction in income taxes when there is investment in new facilities. The procedure is to calculate income taxes in the usual way, then subtract the investment tax credit, which is some percentage of the investment made that year.

Again there is concern for future generations. But instead of saying that it never happened, as with fast-depreciation tax deferrals, the accounting treatment admits that it happened, but only a little at a time! The whole investment tax credit is deferred in the year in which it occurs; then it is amortized, or taken as a credit, gradually, over a future period of years which is generally equal to the estimated life of the asset in which the investment is made.

As before, the income statement shows the actual income taxes, less investment credit, as paid to the taxing authority. To this is added, as a debit expense, *Deferred Investment Tax Credit.* The offsetting credit entry is to *Accumulated Investment Tax Credit,* which is shown on the liability side of the balance sheet. This is step one. Step two is to amortize, each year, the investment tax credit by a credit entry (reduction of expense) on the income statement called *Amor-*

tization of Investment Tax Credit, equal to $1/n_c$ of the original investment tax credit, where n_c is the amortization period. The offsetting debit is to Accumulated Investment Tax Credit on the balance sheet, by which means it is reduced to zero at the end of the amortization period. The following three statements illustrate this procedure.

Income Tax Statement

Revenues		100
Operating Expenses	41	
Depreciation	16	
Interest on Debt	15	
Total Deductions		72
Taxable Income		28
Tax at 50%		14
Less: 4% Investment Tax Credit		
on 300 Investment		12
Net Tax Payable		2

Operating Statement

Revenues		100
Operating Expenses	41	
Depreciation	10	
Income Taxes	2	
Deferred Income Taxes	3	
Deferred Investment Tax Credit	12	
Less: Amortization of Investment		
Tax Credit ($n_c = 12$)	(1)	
Interest on Debt	15	
Total Expense		82
Net Income		18

Balance Sheet

Assets		Liabilities	
Gross Plant	300	Capital Stock	150
Less: Accumulated		Retained Earnings	18
Depreciation	10	Long-Term Debt	150
Net Plant	290	Accounts Payable	20
Cash	18	Short-Term Loans	30
Accounts Receivable	50	Accumulated Deferred	
Materials Inventory	20	Income Tax	3
Deferred Debits	4	Accumulated Investment	
	382	Tax Credit	11
			382

These statements show the effect of amortizing an investment tax credit in the year in which it occurs. The investment is presumed to be 300, which at a rate of 4% gives a one-time investment tax credit of 12, which is immediately deferred. Simultaneously, one-twelfth of this (assuming a 12-year amortization period) is credited back to the income statement, leaving a net of 11 in the balance sheet at the end of the year as accumulated investment tax credit.

The effect on cash flow is shown by the following statement:

Source and Disposition of Funds

Cash at Beginning of Period		0
Net Income	18	
Depreciation	10	
Deferred Income Taxes	3	
Deferred Investment Tax Credit (Net)	11	
Cash from Operations (Cash Flow)		42
Sale of Capital Stock	150	
New Long-Term Debt	150	
Short-Term Loans	30	
Cash from External Sources		330
Total Funds Available		372
Disposition of Funds:		
Construction Expenditure		300
Net Increase in Working Capital:		
Accounts Receivable	50	
Materials Inventory	20	
Accounts Payable	(20)	50
Deferred Debits		4
Total Funds Dispersed		354
Cash at End of Period		18
		372

Like fast-depreciation tax deferrals, the amortization of investment tax credit creates cash flow and protects future rate-payers; but it is different in that it represents an actual, immediate reduction in tax expense. And again, it is possible, as an alternative procedure, to ignore the amortization process and simply flow through to net income the investment tax credits as they occur.

OTHER ACCOUNTING CONSIDERATIONS

It has been impossible in this brief discussion to cover all aspects of electric utility accounting procedures. There are, however, two further accounting concepts that will require understanding in the later development of generation economic methods. One of these is the Construction Work in Progress account.

Construction Work in Progress

In the very simplified illustrations of accounting operations given earlier, the acquisition of the production plant was by simple cash purchase, all at once. While such a transaction would be possible, it rarely happens because utilities almost universally construct (or finance the construction of) their own generation plants. Construction times are long—measured in years—and with continuously growing electric demand, utilities are continuously constructing plants. This means that they always have substantial funds invested in plant that is not yet productive; and it is common practice to separate on the balance sheet this nonproductive plant investment from the productive, or in-service, plant investment.

This is accomplished by the *Construction Work in Progress* (CWIP) account. As construction expenditures are made (by credit entries to Cash or Accounts Payable), they are accumulated by debits in the CWIP account. When a plant goes into service, its cost is transferred, by credit and debit entries, respectively, from CWIP to Plant. This process is called 'capitalizing' the plant.

In some regulatory jurisdictions, amounts in the CWIP account are not included in the rate base—which is the investment base upon which return is calculated for rate-making purposes. This, in effect, means that the utility is not allowed to earn a return on a substantial amount of investment which it has nevertheless had to finance in order to fulfill its obligation to future electricity users. Whatever the arguments pro and con, the situation has given rise to a procedure of capitalizing the interest expense associated with financing CWIP.

Interest During Construction

It will be recalled that a positive balance in an asset account is a debit, and that a positive balance in an expense account is also a debit. Interest on borrowed funds is normally considered an expense of operation, and this is clear if the borrowed funds are used to provide capital assets, which are the necessary means for production. But—so the argument goes—interest on funds borrowed *during* construction of capital assets, such as generation plant, is actually a part of the investment: the plant could not be constructed without incurring interest expense—just as it could not be constructed without incurring expense for materials and labor. If the latter expense is capitalized, why not the former?

So some portion of actual interest expenditures in each accounting period is counted not as an expense but as an investment in an asset—the plant under construction. The procedure is to charge, each period, a nominal interest percentage of the balance in the CWIP account and add it to the account. Thus, when a plant is completed and capitalized, the interest charged during construction will carry over to the Plant account as part of the total investment (and rate base). This transaction is a debit to CWIP (an increase) and ultimately to Plant. The corresponding credit must logically be to the Interest Expense account (a reduction in actual interest expense).

There is a stigma of long standing attached to the procedure of capitalizing an expense because it was once used, unscrupulously, to 'write up' both assets and profits where the expense had no legitimate relationship to an increase in the value of an asset, e.g. maintenance expense. Consequently, care is taken in preparation of financial reports to reveal the fact that interest during construction has been capitalized. It is the usual practice to show the capitalized interest separately on the income statement, thereby calling attention to its use. This means that the item for interest expense on the income statement is the actual interest paid. But at the end of the statement there is an item, 'Interest During Construction (Cr.),' which appears as a direct adder to net income, but which is conceptually a reduction in interest expense. Sometimes an alternate expression, 'Allowance for Funds Used During Construction,' appears on the income statement, in recognition that some construction funds are provided by equity capital, not interest-bearing loans; but the principle is the same: a nominal percentage is added to CWIP (a debit) and to Net Income (a credit).

This practice, widely accepted and used in the United States, has been criticized as producing 'phantom profits,' or 'low-quality earnings,' although it is sanctioned by regulatory and accounting bodies. There is a trend toward including CWIP in the rate base, so that a return may be earned on it; and this would appear to eliminate the need for continued capitalization of interest during construction.

4

The Time Value of Money

The most familiar expression of the time value of money is the interest that one earns when leaving money on deposit in a bank. Thus, if a depositor places $1 at 6% compound interest for 20 years, he expects at the end of that period to have $1 \times (1.06)^{20} = \$3.21$ available for his use. This is simple enough, but for the purpose of comparing alternate economic plans, there are some additional implications. In deciding to invest his funds at 6% interest, the depositor, in effect, is saying, 'It is a matter of indifference to me whether I have one dollar today or $3.21 twenty years from now.' For a 10-year deposit, his indifference value would be $1.79. The depositor is also saying, 'I have no other use for my funds that will make them produce more than 6% return with acceptable security.' Thus, 6% is *his* time value of money. Another person might have a different idea of the value of his money and would invest it elsewhere.

The point of all this is that a dollar today is not the same as a dollar sometime in the future. Economic analyses of alternate facilities plans normally encompass a period of time that is at least a major fraction of the life of the facilities. Expenditures, both capital and expense, will occur at differing times and in differing amounts for each plan. In totting up for comparison, it is essential that the differences in timing be recognized. Hence the time value of money *must* be included in any proper economic analysis. Otherwise, no rational conclusions can be drawn.

It is thus necessary to develop means for 'moving' money in time, and this of course introduces the subject of interest formulas.

RETURN, INTEREST, AND DISCOUNT

Return is the generic yield, or profit, on an investment. Interest is 'money paid for the use of money.' In the context of the corporation, it is the fixed return paid to bondholders. There is no special term for return to shareholders—it is called just that, or 'equity return.' It consists of retained earnings and dividends paid.

In banking terms, a discount is interest paid in advance on a loan, and the discount rate is the rate of interest used. In a more general financial sense, and as used in this book, it is the time value of money to be used for moving money in time. It may be equal to an interest rate or to a weighted average of returns to bondholders and stockholders, and it may or may not reflect an adjustment for the effect of income taxes, as will be explained in Chapter 5.

In the following development of interest formulas, the term 'interest' is used because it is traditional. The appropriate value to use in the formulas, however, is the discount rate, whatever its definition may be in a specific instance.

SINGLE–PAYMENT INTEREST FACTORS

The increasing value in time of a single payment, or amount of money, is measured by compound interest. An amount P at the beginning of year 1 has, at the end of year n, a value S given by the following expression:

$$S = P(1 + r)^n, \tag{4.1}$$

where r is the interest rate in per unit.

The factor $(1 + r)^n$ is called the compound-amount factor. It is thought of as the factor required to move a sum, or payment, *forward* in time n years. The reciprocal is known as the present-worth factor (PWF):

$$\text{PWF} = \frac{1}{(1 + r)^n}. \tag{4.2}$$

The present-worth factor moves a payment *backward* in time n years. The name 'present worth,' or present value, derives from the most common operation—moving a future payment back to the present time; but of course the movement can be to any year—present, past or future. In this case it avoids confusion to specify, by saying, 'present worth as of _____year.' This is the parlance even though the reference year may be in the future. The expression 'future worth' is sometimes used.

Since a year is not a point in time but a period of time, it is important to note the necessary and universal convention regarding beginning- and end-of-year payments. A present worth, or an investment,* P, is made at the beginning of a designated year; interest and other expenses are paid at the end of year, and the compound amount, S, is also at the end of year. Thus the compound amount in 1980 is numerically equal to the present worth as of 1981.

---

* In terms of interest formulas, 'present worth' and 'investment' are the same thing. In generation economic analyses, they are generally not. See below, p. 59.

SERIES INTEREST FACTORS

In economic analysis it is frequently desired to find the aggregate present worth of a time series of numbers as of some particular year. If the series is nonuniform and without any mathematical pattern, it is necessary to treat each element as a single payment and move it separately in time to the desired year. The sum of the individual present-worth values is the present worth of the series:

$$P = \sum_{1}^{n} \frac{R(y)}{(1 + r)^y}, \tag{4.3}$$

where P = present worth, beginning of year 1.

$R(y)$ = payment in year y (end of year).

If the series is uniform, or of arithmetic or geometric form, simple formulas may be used to obtain the present worth.

Uniform Series

A uniform series of end-of-year payments, R, has a present worth, as of the first year of the series.

$$P = R\left[\frac{1}{1 + r} + \frac{1}{(1 + r)^2} + \frac{1}{(1 + r)^3} + \cdots \frac{1}{(1 + r)^n}\right]. \tag{4.4}$$

Multiplying both sides of the equation by $(1 + r)$,

$$(1 + r)P = R\left[1 + \frac{1}{1 + r} + \frac{1}{(1 + r)^2} + \cdots \frac{1}{(1 + r)^{n-1}}\right]. \tag{4.5}$$

Subtracting (4.5) from (4.4):

$$P(1 - 1 - r) = R\left[\frac{1}{(1 + r)^n} - 1\right],$$

and,

$$P = R\left[\frac{1 - \dfrac{1}{(1 + r)^n}}{r}\right] = R\left[\frac{(1 + r)^n - 1}{r(1 + r)^n}\right]. \tag{4.6}$$

The factor by which R is multiplied is called the uniform-series present-worth factor, but it is more commonly used in its inverse form, which is known as the capital recovery factor (CRF):

$$\text{CRF} = \frac{r(1 + r)^n}{(1 + r)^n - 1}; \tag{4.7}$$

$$R = P(\text{CRF}). \tag{4.8}$$

The CRF is so-called because it is the factor that, applied to an investment (the present worth), gives the uniform annual end-of-year payment required to provide recovery *of* the investment together with return (interest) *on* the investment. It is, for example, the factor used to calculate monthly mortgage payments, where n is the number of months, and r the monthly interest rate, normally taken as one-twelfth of the quoted annual rate.

The sinking-fund factor (SFF) may be derived as follows: From eqn (4.1),

$$P = \frac{S}{(1 + r)^n}. \tag{4.9}$$

Substituting in eqn (4.8),

$$R = S \frac{(CRF)}{(1 + r)^n} = S \frac{r}{(1 + r)^n - 1} = S(SFF); \tag{4.10}$$

$$SFF = \frac{r}{(1 + r)^n - 1}. \tag{4.11}$$

The sinking-fund factor determines the uniform annual payment, R, which will amount to a desired future value, S. It can be shown algebraically that,

$$CRF = SFF + r. \tag{4.12}$$

In this form, the CRF annual payment is interpreted to be in two parts: the SFF which in n years will provide the recovery *of* the investment; and r, which provides the annual return *on* the investment.

Both the single-payment and uniform-series interest factors can be found in standard interest tables. The terminology is variable. The single-payment PWF is sometimes called the compound discount factor; a uniform annual series may be called an annuity.

Geometric Series

Not found in most interest tables, but useful nevertheless, is the present worth of a geometric series. It is sometimes called an inflation series, because that is its most common expression. A geometric series of n terms may be of the form:

$$1, 1 + u, (1 + u)^2, \cdots (1 + u)^{n-1}, \tag{4.13}$$

where u is the annual inflation rate. By algebraic operations similar to those used to derive the present worth of a uniform series, the following expressions may be obtained:

$$P = \frac{1 - \left(\dfrac{1 + u}{1 + r}\right)^n}{r - u}, \tag{4.14}$$

where $u \neq r$, and

$$P = \frac{n}{1 + r}, \tag{4.15}$$

where $u = r$.

The second form of the equation is given only for mathematical completeness: in usual economic theory, the acceptable interest rate, r, is the sum of a basic 'rental' value of money (3% or 4%) and the anticipated rate of future inflation. Thus it is not logically possible for u to equal r.

The most common use of the present worth of an inflation series is to convert it to an equivalent uniform series by multiplying P by the CRF.

Arithmetic Series

Occasionally useful is the n-element arithmetic series,

$$0, g, 2g, 3g, \cdots (n - 1)g, \tag{4.16}$$

where g is the common difference, or gradient. The present worth is

$$P = \frac{g}{r}\left[\frac{1}{\mathrm{CRF}} - \frac{n}{(1 + r)^n}\right]. \tag{4.17}$$

The uniform equivalent, R, is $P(\mathrm{CRF})$, or

$$R = \frac{g}{r}[1 - n(\mathrm{SFF})]. \tag{4.18}$$

Product of Arithmetic and Geometric Series

In approximate comparisons of individual generating units, it is useful to know the uniform equivalent of the product of fuel cost, which is frequently taken to be a geometric series, and capacity factor, which may be represented as a negative arithmetic series, thus:

$$F(1)C_f(1), \ F(1)(1 + u)[C_f(1) - g], \ F(1)(1 + u)^2[C_f(1) - 2g], \cdots$$
$$\cdots F(1)(1 + u)^{n-1}[C_f(1) - (n - 1)g],$$

where $F(1)$ = fuel cost, year 1, and $C_f(1)$ = capacity factor, year 1.

The present worth of this series is:

$$P = F(1)C_f(1)\left\{\frac{1 - k^n}{r - u} - \frac{g}{C_f(1)}\left[\frac{k - nk^n + (n - 1)k^{n+1}}{(r - u)(1 - k)}\right]\right\}, \tag{4.19}$$

where $k = (1 + u)/(1 + r)$. If the arithmetic series is positive, rather than negative, the sign preceding the factor $g/C_f(1)$ changes to plus.

The uniform annual equivalent, R, is the product of P and the CRF.

SUMMARY OF INTEREST FORMULAS

Single Payment

$$PWF = \frac{1}{(1 + r)^n}$$

$$P = S(PWF)$$

Uniform Series

$$CRF = \frac{r(1 + r)^n}{(1 + r)^n - 1}$$

$$R = P(CRF)$$

$$SFF = \frac{r}{(1 + r)^n - 1}$$

$$R = S(SFF)$$

Geometric Series

$$P = \frac{1 - \left(\dfrac{1 + u}{1 + r}\right)^n}{r - u}$$

Arithmetic Series

$$P = \frac{g}{r}\left[\frac{1}{(CRF)} - \frac{n}{(1 + r)^n}\right]$$

$$R = \frac{g}{r}[1 - n(SFF)]$$

Series of Geometric and Arithmetic Products

$$P = F(1)C_f(1)\left\{\frac{1 - k^n}{r - u} \pm \frac{g}{C_f(1)}\left[\frac{k - nk^n + (n - 1)k^{n+1}}{(r - u)(1 - k)}\right]\right\}$$

$$k = (1 + u)/(1 + r).$$

5

Revenue Requirements: The Fixed-Charge Rate

Decisions relating to the investment in new facilities in any kind of industry involve the answering of two questions: 'Shall new facilities be obtained?'; and, 'If so, which new facilities should be selected?' In electric utility generation, the former question may arise in the decision to retire existing units and replace them. But the great majority of generation decisions involve no choice as to whether new facilities should be provided—the system load is growing and new capacity is a must. The only question is, 'what kind?' This relative absence of 'opportunity investment,' and the fact that the utility industry is very capital-intensive and regulated with respect to revenues, may be the reason why the Revenue Requirements method of economic analysis is most widely used. Major emphasis, therefore, will be placed on this method, although brief discussions of the Payback, Net Present Worth, and Discounted Cash Flow methods commonly used in other industries are included in Chapter 6.

REVENUE REQUIREMENTS METHOD

Table 5.1 is a typical income statement for an investor-owned utility, complete but simplified for the purpose of deriving the annual revenue requirement. It will be helpful to think of this statement as representing a (highly improbable) company with one generating plant, which was constructed all at one time and will be retired all at one time after n years with zero salvage value. From the last line of the income statement,

$$R_1(y) = \text{Rev}(y) - E(y) - D(y) - A(y) - T(y) + I(y) - R_2(y), \quad (5.1)$$

where $R_1(y)$, $\text{Rev}(y)$, and so on, are the annual values for year y, as defined in Table 5.1.

Table 5.1. Income statement (using flow-through accounting).

Revenue		$\text{Rev}(y)$
Less:	Production Cost	$E(y)$
	Depreciation	$D(y)$
	Ad Valorem Taxes and Insurance	$A(y)$
	Income Tax Paid*	$T(y) - I(y)$
Operating Income		$\text{Rev}(y) - E(y) - D(y) - A(y)$ $- T(y) + I(y)$
Less:	Interest (return) on bonds	$R_2(y)$
Net Income (Equity Return)		$R_1(y) = \text{Rev}(y) - E(y) - D(y)$ $- A(y) - T(y) + I(y) - R_2(y)$

* $T(y)$ = Income Tax
 $I(y)$ = Investment Tax Credit

This is the real-time accounting equation, used to calculate net income, or return to the equity investors, after the investment has been made, the plant operated, expenses incurred, and revenues received. The equation could just as logically be used for future-time, where the problem is to decide which among alternate generation investments is most advantageous. This would require estimating future values of expenses and revenues for each alternate, then calculating equity return which would be the criterion of economic choice; i.e. the alternate with the highest estimated equity return would be the choice.

This is something like the procedure of financial simulation, a method which is limited to total system analyses, described in a subsequent chapter. The method is not used for single-unit analyses because it requires an estimate of future revenues, which is difficult, at best, and somewhat meaningless, too, when considered with respect to a single asset that is only a small part of the assets of a total enterprise. So the equation is turned around as follows:

$$\text{Rev}(y) = R_1(y) + R_2(y) + E(y) + A(y) + D(y) + T(y) - I(y). \quad (5.2)$$

$\text{Rev}(y)$ now becomes the *revenue requirement* for producing a minimum acceptable return, $R_1(y) + R_2(y)$, given known or estimated values of the other variables. The criterion of economic choice is the lowest revenue requirement because, regardless of what the actual revenues turn out to be, the alternate having the lowest revenue requirement will always produce the greatest return (or least loss).

All of the components of $\text{Rev}(y)$ except $E(y)$ are directly proportional to the capital investment. Once the investment has been made, these revenue requirements are committed and unavoidable. They are not actually 'fixed' in the sense of being constant, but taken together, they are commonly called *fixed charges*. The production cost $E(y)$, which includes fuel, labor, and materials, is a variable revenue requirement because its magnitude depends primarily on the amount of future operation of the plant, not on the mere fact of an investment having been made.

The total annual revenue requirements of a project, then, are the fixed charges on the capital investment plus the annual operating, or production, expenses. Although it is not conceptually correct to refer to revenue requirements as 'costs,' this is very commonly done for ease of expression, it being understood that the Revenue Requirements method is being used.

Methods of obtaining annual production costs will be developed in another chapter; the pages that follow discuss methods of calculating the fixed-charges component of total costs.

YEARLY FIXED–CHARGE RATE

The fixed-charge rate is the annual fraction which, when applied to the initial plant investment, will give the annual revenue requirement for capital. If the initial investment in dollars is taken as P', and the variables of eqn (5.2) redefined to be fractional multipliers of P' instead of absolute dollars,

$$\text{FCR}(y)P' = [R_1(y) + R_2(y) + D(y) + T(y) - I(y) + A(y)]P', \quad (5.3)$$

where $\text{FCR}(y)$ is the per unit fixed-charge rate. As noted above, $E(y)$ is omitted because it is not a direct function of P'. Expressions will now be developed for each of the components of the equation, from which the value of the total fixed-charge rate may be calculated. This will be done in two steps: first the yearly values, which decline through the life of the plant; then the equivalent uniform, or level, values for all combinations of flow-through and normalization of tax deferrals.

Return

If the returns to stockholders, $R_1(y)$, and to bondholders, $R_2(y)$, are combined, the result is the total, or overall, return on the investment. The use of this total return is convenient with respect to the rate regulation function in investor-owned utilities because rates are commonly adjusted to produce a stated allowable return on investment, which includes both shareholders' and bondholders' returns. However, it is *not* this 'allowed' return that is significant in the economic decisions that utility management must make. It is the return required to produce, in the financial markets, the new capital funding needed to maintain the enterprise. The return allowed by the regulatory body may be equal to or less than this, depending on the regulatory body's policies and/or its confidence in the ability of utility management efficiently to supply the public with electric power. But regardless, management must make its choice of facilities investments based on the realities of financial life; and this means using a return which is the minimum acceptable to the shareholders and bondholders of the particular utility at the time.

Determining this Minimum Acceptable Return (MAR) with respect to bondholders is fairly straightforward: examine the current rates of bond interest of the utility involved, or of others having similar financial ratings. Finding an appropriate MAR for equity investors is more involved. It is not the ratio of current earnings to market price, because that reflects the requirements of prospective new shareholders. What is desired is the MAR of pre-project shareholders, the investors whose equity and earnings must be protected. In practice, this MAR is not very different from the ratio of current return to book value of equity capital. For further discussion of this question, see Jeynes (1968).

The rate of MAR is designated i—to be applied to the investors' committed capital. Because of the recovery of investment by annual depreciation charges, this committed capital, or *net plant,* declines each year of the life of the investment, as shown in Table 5.2 for a plant of 10-year life, initial investment of 100, and straight-line depreciation method.

The return on net investment is given mathematically by

$$P'[R_1(y) + R_2(y)] = i\left[P' - P'\sum_0^{y-1} D(x)\right],\qquad(5.4)$$

where $D(x)$ is the annual depreciation charge (Chapter 3) and $D(0) = 0$.

In real terms, the accumulated depreciation is not usually returned to the investors, but is retained in the enterprise for reinvestment in other facilities. When thought of in this way, the return on the initial investment may be considered constant, but partially offset by the growing return on the reinvested accumulated depreciation. The result of this 'net return' concept is the same as of the net plant concept, as shown by a comparison of the last columns of Tables 5.2 and 5.3.

The concept of net return will be found more useful than that of net plant in later development, so it will be used henceforth. It means, in effect, that the current project under consideration is relieved from the responsibility of earning the total return, i, because it produces funds in the form of depreciation which become part of the capital investment in other projects. The return earned on these funds by the other projects is rightfully credited to the current project. To indicate the distinction between net plant and net return, the following form of the expression for overall net return will be used:

$$P'[R_1(y) + R_2(y)] = P'\left[i - i\sum_0^{y-1} D(x)\right].\qquad(5.5)$$

The quantity P', the plant investment in dollars, will be omitted from future expressions because it is always a factor of both sides of the equations.

Depreciation

The depreciation component of the fixed-charge rate is simply the annual value for the various depreciation methods described in Chapter 3.

Income Tax

Income tax refers to the tax levied by governmental bodies on net income—i.e. income belonging to the stockholders, whether paid to them in dividends or not. At first thought, it may seem odd to consider expressing income tax as a

Table 5.2. Return on net plant.

Year	Annual Depreciation*	Accumulated Depreciation†	Net Plant†	Return on Net Plant† MAR = 0.1
1	10	0	100	10
2	10	10	90	9
3	10	20	80	8
4	10	30	70	7
5	10	40	60	6
6	10	50	50	5
7	10	60	40	4
8	10	70	30	3
9	10	80	20	2
10	10	90	10	1

* Charged at *end* of year.
† Balance *during* year.

percentage, or fraction, of investment, since basically it is calculated as a percentage of net income. However, since we are beginning with the assumption of minimum acceptable return and have above calculated overall net return and hence net income as a function of investment, we can in turn calculate income tax as a function of investment also.

The investment tax credit, $I(y)$, is a function of investment by statutory definition. After income taxes are determined in the usual way, a one-time credit of KP' is allowed in the year the plant goes into service. This credit, designed to encourage investment in new plants, may involve values of K up to 10% or more.

Table 5.4 shows the calculation of taxable income and income tax where t is the statutory tax rate. The tax depreciation, D_t, is differentiated from the 'book' depreciation, D, used in the shareholders' income statement because it may be based on a different depreciation method and a different depreciation life. Reasons for choosing one or another method for book depreciation may

Table 5.3. Net return on initial plant.

Year	Accumulated Depreciation	MAR on Initial Investment	MAR on Accumulated Depreciation	Net Return on Initial Investment
1	0	10	0	10
2	10	10	1	9
3	20	10	2	8
4	30	10	3	7
5	40	10	4	6
6	50	10	5	5
7	60	10	6	4
8	70	10	7	3
9	80	10	8	2
10	90	10	9	1

Table 5.4. Income tax statement.

Revenue		$Rev(y)$
Less:	General Expense	$E(y)$
	Depreciation (for tax purposes)	$D_t(y)$
	Interest (return) on bonds	$R_2(y)$
	Ad Valorem Taxes and Insurance	$A(y)$
Taxable Income		$I_t(y) = Rev(y) - E(y)$
		$\quad - D_t(y) - R_2(y) - A(y)$
Income Tax		$T(y) = t[Rev(y) - E(y)$
		$\quad - D_t(y) - R_2(y) - A(y)]$
Less:	Investment Tax Credit	$I(y)$
Net Income Tax Paid		$T(y) - I(y)$

include tradition, rules of governmental regulatory bodies, and whether certain policies are believed to be conservative or progressive, or are held to be peculiar to a particular utility management or accounting milieu. Book depreciation lives are estimated, and occasionally adjusted to correspond to experienced physical lives.

Tax depreciation methods and lives, however, are ordinarily selected for only one purpose: to minimize the impact of income tax. Methods such as SYD and double-rate declining balance produce high depreciation rates in early life and low rates near the end of life. Total accumulated depreciation is, of course, the same under any method; and so, therefore, is the total income tax deduction and the total taxes paid over the life of the asset. But with a high early depreciation method, a portion of the tax liability is deferred; and this, because of the time value of money, effectively reduces the impact of the tax relative to that incurred with SL depreciation. These fast depreciation methods are sometimes referred to as liberalized depreciation. Another way of reducing corporate income taxes without changing the actual tax rate is the use of so-called guideline lives. Guideline lives are depreciation lives for various categories of assets, permissible for income tax purposes, and considerably shorter than reasonably-to-be-expected physical lives. Like liberalized depreciation methods, they produce higher early depreciation charges which defer tax payments.

As a measure of the magnitude of the tax saving resulting from fast depreciation and short lives, consider a case where the book depreciation method is SL and the life 35 years, while the tax depreciation is SYD and the life 20 years. The present worth of the book depreciation at 10% discount rate is

$$P = \frac{1}{n} \times \frac{1}{(CRF)_{n,r}} = \frac{1}{35} \times \frac{1}{0.10369} = 0.276, \tag{5.6}$$

where $(CRF)_{n,r}$ is the capital recovery factor for n years and discount rate r. The present worth of SYD depreciation is given by

$$P = \frac{2}{(CRF)_{m,r}(m + 1)r} \left[(CRF)_{m,r} - \frac{1}{m} \right], \tag{5.7}$$

where m = tax depreciation life; thus

$$P = \frac{2}{0.11746 \times 21 \times 0.1}\left(0.11746 - \frac{1}{20}\right) = 0.547. \qquad (5.8)$$

Considering the time value of money, the tax depreciation, hence the tax deduction, is nearly twice that for books.

In order to derive the revenue requirement for income tax, the taxable income must be expressed in terms of the equity return, R_1. Using the development of Table 5.4, and again redefining the variables as yearly fractions to be applied to the initial investment, taxable income is

$$I_t(y) = \text{Rev}(y) - E(y) - D_t(y) - R_2(y) - A(y). \qquad (5.9)$$

Substituting $\text{Rev}(y)$ from eqn (5.2),

$$I_t(y) = R_1(y) - D_t(y) + D(y) + T(y) - I(y). \qquad (5.10)$$

Income tax is the tax rate, t, times taxable income, giving

$$T(y) = t[R_1(y) - D_t(y) + D(y) + T(y) - I(y)]. \qquad (5.11)$$

Solving,

$$T(y) = \frac{t}{1 - t}[R_1(y) - D_t(y) + D(y) - I(y)]. \qquad (5.12)$$

From eqn (5.5), the net overall return is

$$R_1(y) + R_2(y) = i - i\sum_0^{y-1} D(x). \qquad (5.13)$$

If the bond interest rate is designated as b, and the proportion of bond financing to total financing (debt ratio) as B, then the proportion of net return belonging to bondholders is $\dfrac{bB}{i}$ and that to shareholders $\left(1 - \dfrac{bB}{i}\right)$. Thus, from eqn (5.13),

$$R_1(y) = \left[i - i\sum_0^{y-1} D(x)\right]\left(1 - \frac{bB}{i}\right). \qquad (5.14)$$

Substituting (5.14) in (5.12) gives

$$T(y) = \frac{t}{1 - t}\left\{\left[i - i\sum_0^{y-1} D(x)\right]\left(1 - \frac{bB}{i}\right) - D_t(y) + D(y) - I(y)\right\}. \qquad (5.15)$$

As noted above, the investment tax credit $I(y)$ has the value K in year 1 and zero in all other years. The final expression for $T(y)$ is:

$$T(y) = \frac{t}{1-t}\left\{\left[i - i\sum_0^{y-1}D(x)\right]\left(1 - \frac{bB}{i}\right) - D_t(y) + D(y) - KZ(y)\right\},$$

(5.16)

where $Z(y) = 1$ for $y = 1$
$\qquad = 0$ for $y > 1$.

Note that this equation includes the investment tax credit only because it is a part of the net income of Table 5.1 but is not taxable. The true net income tax liability is $T(y) - KZ(y)$, but since investment tax credit has been shown separately in Table 5.1 and eqn (5.3), it will not be considered as a part of $T(y)$, but will be included when the total fixed-charge rate is summed.

Ad Valorem Taxes and Insurance

There is no general rule governing the annual per unit values for ad valorem taxes and insurance. They are frequently used as level or equal annual values during the life of the plant, but each specific situation must be investigated to obtain the proper values. Not all types of generating units necessarily have the same insurance requirements. Extra liability insurance may be necessary for nuclear units, for example.

Total Yearly Fixed-Charge Rate: Flow-Through

The total fixed-charge rate is the sum of the revenue requirements for return, depreciation, income tax, ad valorem tax, and insurance, less investment tax credit, as defined by eqn (5.3).

$$Return = i - i\sum_0^{y-1}D(x)$$

$$+ \; Depreciation = D(y)$$

$$+ \; Income\ Tax = \frac{t}{1-t}\left\{\left(1 - \frac{bB}{i}\right)\left[i - i\sum_0^{y-1}D(x)\right]\right.$$
$$\left. - D_t(y) + D(y) - KZ(y)\right\}$$

$$+ \; Ad\ Valorem\ Taxes\ and\ Insurance = A(y)$$

$$- \; Investment\ Tax\ Credit = KZ(y),$$

(5.17)

where $Z(y) = 1$ for $y = 1$
$\qquad = 0$ for $y > 1$.

Total Yearly Fixed-Charge Rate: Normalized

It will be recalled from Chapter 3 that the normalization procedure applies to the treatment of tax deferrals on the income statement; the calculation of tax paid is the same for either flow-through or normalization. Hence the income tax statement of Table 5.4 remains applicable, but a new income statement, Table 5.5, is required for developing the fixed-charge rate, normalized. From this table,

$$FCR(y) = R_1(y) + R_2(y) + D(y) + T(y) + T_d(y) - I_a(y) + A(y). \quad (5.18)$$

Note that the investment tax credit, $I(y)$, does not appear because it is deferred as soon as received: its effect is completely expressed by the annual amortization $I_a(y)$. The deferred income tax $T_d(y)$ is the result of the varying differences between the methods and timing of book and tax depreciation as described in Chapter 3.

The expression for the yearly fixed-charge rate, normalized, may be developed from eqn (5.18) by a procedure similar to that of the flow-through case. It is given below:

$$Return = i\left\{ 1 - \sum_0^{y=1} D(x) - t \sum_0^{y=1} [D_t(x) - D'(x)] - K\left(1 - \frac{y-1}{n_c}\right)Q(y)\right\}$$

$$+ \; Depreciation = D(y)$$

$$+ \; Income\ Tax = \frac{t}{1-t}\left\{\left(1 - \frac{bB}{i}\right)(Return\ as\ above)\right.$$

$$\left. - D_t(y) + D(y) + t[D_t(y) - D'(y)] - \frac{KW(y)}{n_c}\right\}$$

$$+ \; Deferred\ Income\ Tax = t[D_t(y) - D'(y)]$$

Table 5.5. Income statement (using normalized accounting).

Revenue		$Rev(y)$
Less:	Production Cost	$E(y)$
	Depreciation	$D(y)$
	Ad Valorem Taxes and Insurance	$A(y)$
	Income Tax Paid	$T(y) - I(y)$
	Deferred Investment Tax Credit	$I(y)$
	Deferred Income Tax	$T_d(y)$
Add:	Amortization of Investment Tax Credit	$I_a(y)$
Operating Income		$Rev(y) - E(y) - D(y) - A(y)$ $- T(y) - T_d(y) + I_a(y)$
Less:	Interest (return) on bonds	$R_2(y)$
Net Income		$R_1(y) = Rev(y) - E(y)$ $- D(y) - R_2(y) - A(y)$ $- T(y) - T_d(y) + I_a(y)$

$$- \text{ Amortized Investment Tax Credit } = \frac{KW(y)}{n_c}$$

$$+ \text{ Ad Valorem Taxes and Insurance } = A(y), \qquad (5.19)$$

where $Q(y) = 0$ for $y = 1$

$\qquad\qquad = 0$ for $y > n_c$

$\qquad\qquad = 1$ for $1 < y = n_c$

$\quad W(y) = 1$ for $y \leq n_c$

$\qquad\qquad = 0$ for $y > n_c$

$\qquad n_c =$ amortization period for investment tax credit

$\qquad D'(y) =$ depreciation for normalizing.

The annual deferred income tax is the tax rate times the difference between tax depreciation and some other, 'slower' depreciation, $D'(y)$. In *full* normalization, this other depreciation is that calculated using the book method and book life; i.e., $D'(y) = D(y)$. In *partial* normalization, the other depreciation is that calculated using the book method, but tax life. The effect of partial normalization is to defer the tax saving resulting from difference in the method of depreciation but to flow through that resulting from difference in life. Other combinations are, of course, possible.

LEVELING THE FIXED–CHARGE RATE

The declining yearly fixed-charge rate derivations just given are very helpful in understanding the principles of the Revenue Requirements method; but yearly values are cumbersome to work with and really necessary only in some kinds of total system analyses. In direct unit evaluations, the present worth of revenue requirements is a frequent criterion of choice; and for this purpose a level fixed-charge rate is far simpler to use. A level fixed-charge-rate series has, of course, the same present worth as the actual declining yearly series; and it may be expressed as follows:

$$\text{fcr} = (\text{CRF})_{n,r} \sum_{1}^{n} \left[\frac{\text{FCR}(y)}{(1 + r)^y} \right], \qquad (5.20)$$

where $(\text{CRF})_{n,r} =$ the capital recovery factor for n years at rate r.

$\qquad \text{fcr} =$ level fixed-charge rate

$\qquad \text{FCR}(y) =$ yearly fixed-charge rate

$\qquad r =$ discount rate

$\qquad n =$ life, or amortization period.

There is no unanimity of opinion as to the correct value of the discount rate, r, to be used for leveling the fixed-charge rate (or for present-worth calculations in general). In one school are those who use the internal rate of return, or after-tax rate, i-tbB (Bary and Brown, 1957). Jeynes (1968) and others maintain that the proper discount rate is simply the overall rate of return, i, or MAR. Since practice among utilities—in the United States, at least—is divided, the expressions for level fixed-charge rate under alternate tax-accounting assumptions will first be developed generically, using discount rate r. The effects of alternate values i, or i-tbB, will then be given.

LEVEL FIXED–CHARGE RATE: FLOW–THROUGH

The equations will be developed by components, as with the yearly fixed-charge rate. Level quantities will be distinguished by the use of lower-case letters; e.g. d is the level equivalent of $D(y)$.

Return

Referring to eqn (5.5), the annual net return is i less the return on accumulated depreciation. The return, i, is already in level form. The level return on accumulated depreciation is i times the level equivalent of accumulated depreciation. Mathematically, the net return on equity and debt is:

$$(r_1 + r_2) = i(1 - a_d),\tag{5.21}$$

where a_d = level equivalent of accumulated depreciation, which may be evaluated as follows.

If the annual depreciation charges were accumulated to end of life at $r = 0$, the sum would be unity:

$$\sum_1^n D(y) = 1.0.\tag{5.22}$$

If the equivalent level annual depreciation charges are accumulated at interest rate r, the amount is:

$$S = \frac{d}{(\text{SFF})_{n,r}},\tag{5.23}$$

by definition of d (the r-leveled value of depreciation) and SFF. The aggregate amount of the interest, at rate r, on accumulated depreciation at the end of n years, must be the difference, or

$$\text{Accumulated Interest} = \frac{d}{(\text{SFF})_{n,r}} - 1.\tag{5.24}$$

The level equivalent of this interest sum is obtained by multiplying by the SFF, giving,

$$\text{Level Equivalent Interest} = d - (\text{SFF})_{n,r}.\tag{5.25}$$

This level equivalent of interest on accumulated depreciation is also the product of the rate, r, and the level equivalent of accumulated depreciation, a_d. Hence,

$$ra_d = d - (SFF)_{n,r},$$

(5.26)

and

$$a_d = \frac{d}{r} - \frac{(SFF)_{n,r}}{r}.$$

(5.27)

Substituting in eqn (5.21), the level net return is

$$r_1 + r_2 = i - \frac{i}{r}[d - (SFF)_{n,r}].$$

(5.28)

Depreciation

Each of the depreciation methods discussed in Chapter 3 may be expressed as an equivalent level value. Straight-line depreciation is, of course, inherently level:

$$d = \frac{1}{m}\frac{(CRF)_{n,r}}{(CRF)_{m,r}},$$

(5.29)

where m is the depreciation life, and n the amortization period, or book life, which may be different from m. Expressions for other depreciation methods are given below. Derivations may be found in Heck (1961).

The equation for level *sinking-fund* depreciation is:

$$d = (SFF)_{m,j}\left[\frac{1 - \left(\dfrac{1+j}{1+r}\right)^m}{r - j}\right](CRF)_{n,r},$$

(5.30)

where j = sinking-fund interest rate, and $j \neq r$;

$$d = (SFF)_{m,r}\left(\frac{m}{1+r}\right)(CRF)_{n,r},$$

(5.31)

where $j = r$.

For *SYD depreciation:*

$$d = \frac{2}{r(1+m)}\left[(CRF)_{m,r} - \frac{1}{m}\right]\frac{(CRF)_{n,r}}{(CRF)_{m,r}}.$$

(5.32)

For *Declining Balance* depreciation:

$$d = (CRF)_{n,r}\left\{\frac{f}{r+f}\left[1 - \left(\frac{1-f}{1+r}\right)^q\right] + \left(\frac{1-f}{1+r}\right)^q\frac{1}{(m-q)(CRF)_{m-q,r}}\right\},$$

(5.33)

where f = rate applied to declining balance
q = year before switch to straight-line on remaining balance.

Income Tax

Referring to eqn (5.16), the annual value of income tax, the only component not yet leveled, is the investment tax credit, K. This, it will be recalled, is a one-time credit at the end of year 1. Its present worth is $\dfrac{K}{1 + r}$, and the uniform equivalent annual value is this times the capital recovery factor, or

$$\frac{K(\text{CRF})_{n,r}}{1 + r}.$$

The expression for the total level revenue requirement for income tax, $\bar{T}$, is

$$\bar{T} = \frac{t}{1 - t}\left[\left(1 - \frac{bB}{i}\right)\left\{i - \frac{i}{r}[d - (\text{SFF})_{n,r}]\right\} - (d_t - d) - \frac{K(\text{CRF})_{n,r}}{1 + r}\right].$$

$$(5.34)$$

This result has been obtained through long derivation and much mathematical manipulation. It can be understood logically, however, by recognizing that the equation starts with MAR ($= i$) and progressively adjusts and corrects it to obtain taxable income, to which it then applies the tax rate, as follows:

The expression $\left\{i - \dfrac{i}{r}[d - (\text{SFF})_{n,r}]\right\}$ is MAR less the return on the depreciation reserve, which need not be earned by this current investment. It is only the return on equity that is taxable; so $\left(1 - \dfrac{bB}{i}\right)$ factors out the equity portion.

This leaves a net equity return that has been based on book depreciation; so $-(d_t - d)$ substitutes tax depreciation. Similarly,

$$- \frac{K(\text{CRF})_{n,r}}{1 + r}$$

corrects for the fact that equity net return (Table 5.1) included the investment tax credit, which is not taxable as income.

Finally, the entire expression in brackets represents taxable income *after* income tax. Dividing by $(1 - t)$ produces the correct taxable income to which the tax rate is applied.

Total Level Fixed-Charge Rate: Flow Through

Including all of the elements of eqn (5.3), the total level fixed-charge rate is

$$Return = i - \frac{i}{r}[d - (\text{SFF})_{n,r}]$$

$$+ \; Depreciation \; = \; d$$

$$+ \; Income \; Tax \; = \; \frac{t}{1-t}\left\{\left(1 - \frac{bB}{i}\right)(\text{Return}) - (d_t - d) - \frac{K(\text{CRF})_{n,r}}{1+r}\right\}$$

$$- \; Investment \; Tax \; Credit \; = \; \frac{K(\text{CRF})_{n,r}}{1+r}$$

$$+ \; Ad \; Valorem \; Taxes \; and \; Insurance \; = \; a. \tag{5.35}$$

The value for a, ad valorem taxes and insurance, may be originally expressed as level, or it may be calculated from known varying annual values:

$$a = (\text{CRF})_{n,r} \sum_1^n \frac{A(y)}{(1+r)^y}. \tag{5.36}$$

LEVEL FIXED–CHARGE RATE: NORMALIZED

Proceeding from eqn (5.18), the level components of the normalized fixed charge rate will be developed.

Return

The net return is the same as in the flow-through case, except that in addition to return on accumulated depreciation, the current project is credited with two additional items of return: the return on the accumulated deferred income tax, and the return on the accumulated deferred investment tax credit.

The accumulated deferred tax is the tax rate times the cumulative difference between the two depreciation series, which builds up to a maximum near half-life, then declines to zero by the end of life. By reasoning similar to that which developed eqn (5.27), it can be seen that the level value of accumulated difference of two series is the difference between their level values divided by the discount rate. Hence the return on accumulated deferred income taxes is:

$$\frac{i}{r}(td_t - td'),$$

where $d' = d$ for full normalization, or some other value for partial normalization, as described under yearly fixed-charge rate.

The investment tax credit, K, is deferred at the end of year 1. So there is no return earned on deferred investment tax credit during year 1. Also at the end of year 1, K/n_c is credited back into the income statement; so the net value of the deferred investment tax credit during year 2 is

$$K - \frac{K}{n_c}.$$

In each succeeding year, the deferred investment tax credit is reduced by K/n_c.

This thus constitutes a uniform annual series of n_c terms, each being K/n_c. The present worth of this series to the beginning of year 1 is

$$\frac{K}{n_c(\text{CRF})_{n_c,r}},$$

and the level equivalent over investment life n is

$$i_a = \frac{K(\text{CRF})_{n,r}}{n_c(\text{CRF})_{n_c,r}}, \tag{5.37}$$

where i_a = level equivalent of I_a.

The level equivalent of the initially deferred investment tax credit is

$$\frac{K(\text{CRF})_{n,r}}{1+r}.$$

The difference between these two level values is the level equivalent of the return, at rate r, on the accumulated deferred investment tax credit. The return at rate i is:

$$\frac{i}{r}K(\text{CRF})_{n,r}\left[\frac{1}{1+r} - \frac{1}{n_c(\text{CRF})_{n_c,r}}\right].$$

The complete expression for level net return is:

$$r_1 + r_2 = i - \frac{i}{r}\left[d - (\text{SFF})_{n,r} + t(d_t - d')\right.$$

$$\left. + K(\text{CRF})_{n,r}\left(\frac{1}{1+r} - \frac{1}{n_c(\text{CRF})_{n_c,r}}\right)\right]. \tag{5.38}$$

Depreciation

As in the flow-through case, the depreciation is simply d, the level value of book depreciation, defined by one of eqn (5.29) through (5.33).

Income Tax

The equations for income tax (Table 5.4) and net income (Table 5.5) may be solved for income tax, $T(y)$, to give

$$T(y) = \frac{t}{1-t}\{R_1(y) - [D_t(y) - D(y)] + T_d(y) - I_a(y)\}. \tag{5.39}$$

The level equivalent of $R_1(y)$ is $\left(1 - \frac{bB}{i}\right)(r_1 + r_2)$, where $(r_1 + r_2)$ is given by eqn (5.38). The level equivalent of $[D_t(y) - D(y)]$ is $(d_t - d)$, with components defined by eqn (5.29) through (5.33). Similarly, the level equivalent of $T_d(y)$ is $t(d_t - d')$. Equation (5.37) defines i_a, the level equivalent of $I_a(y)$. Thus the equation for the level revenue requirement for income tax is

$$\bar{T} = \frac{t}{1-t}\left[\left(1 - \frac{bB}{i}\right)(r_1 + r_2) - (d_t - d) + t(d_t - d') - \frac{K(CRF)_{n,r}}{n_c(CRF)_{n_c,r}} \right] \quad (5.40)$$

Total Level Fixed-Charge Rate: Normalized

Referring to eqn (5.18), the total level fixed-charge rate, normalized, is

$$Return = i - \frac{i}{r}\left\{ d - (SFF)_{n,r} + t(d_t - d') \right.$$

$$\left. + K(CRF)_{n,r}\left[\frac{1}{1+r} - \frac{1}{n_c(CRF)_{n_c,r}}\right]\right\}$$

$+ Depreciation = d$

$+ Income\ Tax = \dfrac{t}{1-t}\left[\left(1 - \dfrac{bB}{i}\right)(Return\ as\ above) \right.$

$$\left. - (d_t - d) + t(d_t - d') - \frac{K(CRF)_{n,r}}{n_c(CRF)_{n_c,r}} \right]$$

$+ Deferred\ Income\ Tax = t(d_t - d')$

$- Amortized\ Investment\ Tax\ Credit = \dfrac{K(CRF)_{n,r}}{n_c(CRF)_{n_c,r}}$

$+ Ad\ Valorem\ Taxes\ and\ Insurance = a.$ (5.41)

OTHER COMBINATIONS OF TAX TREATMENT

Two other combinations of normalization and flow-through treatment of taxes are possible. The derivation of the fixed-charge-rate expressions is straightforward, using the preceding method, and will not be given here.

Liberalized Depreciation Normalized; Investment Tax Credit Flowed Through

$Return = i - \dfrac{i}{r}[d - (SFF)_{n,r} + t(d_t - d')]$

$+ Depreciation = d$

$+$ *Income Tax* $= \dfrac{t}{1-t} \left\{ \left(1 - \dfrac{bB}{i} \right) \text{(Return as above)} \right.$

$$- (d_t - d) + t(d_t - d') - \frac{K(\text{CRF})_{n,r}}{1+r} \bigg\}$$

$-$ *Investment Tax Credit* $= \dfrac{K(\text{CRF})_{n,r}}{1+r}$

$+$ *Deferred Income Tax* $= t(d_t - d')$

$+$ *Ad Valorem Taxes and Insurance* $= a.$ $\hspace{2cm}$ (5.42)

Liberalized Depreciation Flowed Through; Investment Tax Credit Amortized

Return $= i - \dfrac{i}{r} \left\{ d - (\text{SFF})_{n,r} + K(\text{CRF})_{n,r} \left[\dfrac{1}{1+r} \dfrac{1}{n_c(\text{CRF})_{n_c,r}} \right] \right\}$

$+$ *Depreciation* $= d$

$+$ *Income Tax* $= \dfrac{t}{1-t} \left\{ \left(1 - \dfrac{bB}{i} \right) \text{(Return as above)} - (d_t - d) - \dfrac{K(\text{CRF})_{n,r}}{n_c(\text{CRF})_{n_c,r}} \right\}$

$-$ *Amortized Investment Tax Credit* $= \dfrac{K(\text{CRF})_{n,r}}{n_c(\text{CRF})_{n_c,r}}$

$+$ *Ad Valorem Taxes and Insurance* $= a.$ $\hspace{2cm}$ (5.43)

ALTERNATE DISCOUNT RATES

If the discount rate $r = i$, the effect on eqns (5.35) and (5.41) through (5.43) is clear: the ratio i/r in the expression for return drops out, and all of the level values for depreciation, as well as CRF and SFF, are calculated using i instead of r. The form of the equations does not change.

When, on the other hand, r is taken to be i-tbB, it can be shown that *all four* equations reduce to:

$$\text{fcr} = \frac{(\text{CRF})_{n,r}}{1-t} \left(1 - \frac{K}{1+r} \right) - \frac{td_t}{1-t} + a. \hspace{1cm} (5.44)$$

The absence of book depreciation and the amortization of investment tax credit in this formula, (as well as the fact that the formula is independent of tax accounting method) are explained by noting that these effects are all handled by internal transfers among reserve accounts. They cannot, therefore, influence external cash flows, which over the life of the plant determine the return under the after-tax discount rate philosophy.

The level fixed-charge rate using $i\text{-}tbB$ as discount rate varies from that using i by one percentage point or so, depending on tax accounting method and the values of the parameters. While this is a significant difference, it should be noted that the change in discount rate must also affect the present worth of other costs (fuel, operation, and maintenance) that are part of total revenue requirements. Thus, in an economic study, the choice of discount rate affects both capital and annual production costs, and not necessarily in the same direction. It is difficult to say what the net result will be, but in a comparison among alternates, the effect of discount rate on the economic choice is usually quite small.

NONDEPRECIABLE ASSETS

Some components of the investment in a generating unit, such as land and fuel inventory, may be considered nondepreciable; i.e. they do not wear out, lose their usefulness, or become depleted. The formulas for fixed-charge rate are modified by simply omitting the depreciation components and setting life at infinity. The practical effect of this is that the return component becomes the CRF, which, for $n = \infty$, equals r. Since the investment tax credit is usually disallowed for these types of assets, the value of K in the formulas is set to zero. The result, whether $r = i$, or $r = i - tbB$, is that

$$\text{fcr} = (i - tbB)/(1 - t) + a. \tag{5.45}$$

GOVERNMENT–OWNED UTILITIES

The fixed-charge rate for a government-owned utility is greatly simplified by the elimination of income taxes. The level value is:

$$\text{fcr} = (\text{CRF})_{n,i} + a. \tag{5.46}$$

The overall return, i, will normally be the bond interest rate, b, which is also the discount rate. The value of a may include ad valorem taxes levied by local governments, or it may consist of insurance only.

6
Methods of
Economic Analysis

GENERAL PRINCIPLES

The economic comparison of alternative facilities almost invariably involves alternates whose capital investments and future annual production costs are both different. The problem is to develop for each alternate a single number which can serve as a figure of merit, combining the effects of the cash outlays for capital investment and for annual production expenses. Since the investment has financial implications which extend to the end of the life of the facilities, the analysis must encompass at least a major fraction of that life and, ideally, the whole life. Indeed, some writers recommend calculating an infinite series of costs (which implies perpetual replacement in kind); but the assumptions on which this rationale is based are generally not appropriate to generation equipment. Further, the time value of money makes remote expenditure differences insignificant, in any case. A study period of fifteen to twenty years is usually adequate.

In some kinds of studies it is possible to make what may be called a 'direct unit' comparison, i.e. one without specific reference to the operation or costs of the rest of the generating system. In principle, this is acceptable only if three conditions exist: (1) the total and incremental production costs of the alternates are so nearly equal that one would expect their total energy outputs, based upon economic system dispatch, to be equal; (2) their availabilities are nearly enough equal so that equal energy outputs are physically possible; and (3) their reliabilities, as measured by forced-outage rate and unit size (rating), are equal so that their reserve requirements are equal. In direct unit analyses, costs are calculated as though the generating system consisted only of the one unit in question. Examples of acceptable use of direct unit analysis include the evaluation of units of the same rating having slightly different heat rates, the comparison of alternate methods of auxiliary drive, and the selection of economic condenser-surface area.

Direct unit analysis should not be used for the evaluation of alternate unit sizes, units of markedly different heat rate or reliability characteristics, or units whose fuel prices or escalation factors are different. In such cases, a total system cost analysis is essential—one which, by simulation or other means, recognizes that the operation of the system's other generating units will be affected differently by the different alternates. Total system cost effect is the ultimate criterion. When there is any doubt as to the possible effects on the operation of other generating units, the total system analysis should be made.

In the following discussion of methods of economic analysis, direct unit examples will be given merely for simplicity of illustration. A later chapter will develop the techniques of total system analysis.

REVENUE REQUIREMENTS METHOD: EXAMPLE I

To illustrate the use of the Revenue Requirements method, consider the following example, which for convenience, and to save space, assumes only a five-year life of equipment. For this example, the fcr is leveled with $r = i$.

	Alternate A	Alternate B
Capital Investment	$600 000	$595 000
Life	5 years	5 years
Annual Operating Costs:		
Year 1	60 000	50 000
Year 2	60 000	50 000
Year 3	50 000	50 000
Year 4	25 000	50 000
Year 5	20 000	50 000

The two alternates are considered comparable in reliability and availability, and they will perform the same service over their lifetimes. A direct unit type of comparison is justified. Which alternate is the economic choice?

Fixed-Charge Rate

The first step is to calculate the level fixed-charge rate. The following financial factors are known:

Minimum Acceptable Return	$i = 0.12$
Discount Rate	$r = i = 0.12$
Debt Ratio	$B = 0.5$
Debt Interest Rate	$b = 0.1$
Book Depreciation Life	$n = 5$
Book Depreciation Method	SL

Tax Depreciation Life $\quad\quad\quad m = 4$
Tax Depreciation Method $\quad\quad$ SYD
Investment Tax Credit $\quad\quad\quad K = 0.04$
Tax Accounting Method $\quad\quad$ Flow Through
Income Tax Rate $\quad\quad\quad\quad\quad t = 0.48$
Ad Valorem Tax Rate $\quad\quad\quad a = 0.05$

From these data, the following factors are calculated:

$$(SFF)_n = 0.12/[(1.12)^5 - 1] = 0.15741$$
$$(CRF)_n = 0.12 + 0.15741 = 0.27741$$
$$(CRF)_m = 0.12 + 0.12/[(1.12)^4 - 1] = 0.32923$$
$$d = 1/5 = 0.2$$

From eqn (5.32),

$$d_t = \frac{2}{0.12(5)}\left(0.32923 - \frac{1}{4}\right)\frac{0.27741}{0.32923} = 0.22254.$$

The fixed-charge rate is the sum of the elements given in eqn (5.35):

Return $= 0.12 - (0.2 - 0.15741) = 0.07741$

$+$ *Depreciation* $= 0.2$

$+$ *Income Tax* $= \dfrac{0.48}{0.52}\left[\left(1 - \dfrac{0.1 \times 0.5}{0.12}\right)(0.07741)\right.$

$$\left. - (0.22254 - 0.2) - \frac{0.04(0.27741)}{1.12}\right] = 0.01173$$

$-$ *Investment Tax Credit* $= \dfrac{0.04(0.27741)}{1.12} = 0.00991$

$+$ *Ad Valorem Taxes* $= 0.05.$

The total fixed-charge rate is:

$$fcr = 0.07741 + 0.2 + 0.01173 - 0.00991 + 0.05 = 0.32923.$$

Present Worth of Revenue Requirements

The present worth of the revenue requirement for annual operating costs for Alternate A is:

Year 1	—	60 000/1.12	=	$ 53 571
2	—	60 000/(1.12)² =		47 832
3	—	50 000/(1.12)³ =		35 589
4	—	25 000/(1.12)⁴ =		15 888
5	—	20 000/(1.12)⁵ =		11 348
		TOTAL =		$164 228

To this must be added the present worth of annual revenue requirements for capital (the fixed charges). The uniform annual fixed charges are:

$$600\ 000 \times 0.32923 = 197\ 538,$$

and the present worth is obtained by dividing by the CRF for 5 years and $i = 0.12$:

$$197\ 538/0.27741 = 712\ 080.$$

The present worth of total revenue requirements for Alternate A is

$$164\ 228 + 712\ 080 = 876\ 308.$$

Because the annual operating costs of Alternate B are uniform, their present worth may be calculated directly:

$$50\ 000/0.27741 = 180\ 239.$$

The present worth of fixed charges is:

$$595\ 000 \times \frac{0.32923}{0.27741} = 706\ 146.$$

Alternate B Total Present Worth = 886 385.

Alternate A, having the lower present worth of total revenue requirements, is evidently the economic choice.

Because the Revenue Requirements method frequently compares the present worth of revenue requirements, it is sometimes called the 'present-worth method.' *This is a misnomer* because the use of present worth is merely a convenient way of incorporating the effect of the time value of money—which must be included regardless of method. The characteristic aspect of the Revenue Requirements method is the *fixed-charge rate*, which provides the bridge between a capital investment and annual operating costs. This bridge may be crossed in the opposite direction if desired, thus making a comparison of level annual costs instead of present worth.

Annual Cost Comparison

For Alternate A, the uniform annual operating cost is the present worth times the CRF:

Uniform Annual Operating Cost = 164 228 × 0.27741	= $ 45 558/yr
Fixed Charges	= 197 538
Alternate A Total Annual Cost	$243 096
Similarly, for Alternate B:	
Uniform Annual Operating Cost	= $ 50 000
Fixed Charges	= 195 892
Alternate B Total Annual Cost	$245 892

The relative comparison is the same, and the time value of money is still included because it was necessary to go through the present-worth step to obtain the uniform equivalent annual operating cost for Alternate A.

Capital Investment Comparison

While either the present-worth or annual-cost comparison identifies the economic choice, neither of these conveys much appreciation of the magnitude of the difference, which is typically of the order of only a few percent. A meaningful extension of the calculation is to determine the change in capital investment that would produce an economic standoff. The difference in present worth is:

$$886\ 385 - 876\ 308 = 10\ 077.$$

This has an equivalent uniform annual value of:

$$10\ 077 \times 0.27741 = 2795 \text{ per year.}$$

The capital investment whose fixed charges would equal this annual value is:

$$2795/0.32923 = 8491.$$

Thus, if the capital investment of Alternate B were decreased by 8491, there would be no economic choice; i.e., the break-even investment cost of Alternate B is $595\ 000 - 8491 = 586\ 509$. *Note that present worth of revenue requirements is not the same as capital investment.* The difference in present worth of revenue requirements is 10 007; the equivalent difference in capital cost is 8491. The two could be equal only if fcr = CRF, a situation which requires the absence of all taxes and insurance costs.

REVENUE REQUIREMENTS METHOD: EXAMPLE II

This example will demonstrate the effect of using the fcr leveled at the internal return rate, $i - tbB$, with the same two alternates of Example I. The value of r is now:

$$r = 0.12 - [(0.48)(0.1)(0.5)] = 0.096.$$

The data necessary to calculate the fcr are:

$$(CRF)_{n,r} = 0.26111,$$
$$(CRF)_{m,r} = 0.31274,$$
$$d_t = 0.21827.$$

By eqn (5.44):

$$\text{fcr} = \frac{0.26111}{1 - 0.48}\left(1 - \frac{0.04}{1.096}\right) - \frac{0.48}{0.52}(0.21827) + 0.05$$
$$= 0.33232.$$

Table 6.1. Comparison of discount rates: Revenue Requirements method.

	Example I		Example II
Discount Rate	0.12		0.096
Level Fixed Charge Rate	0.32923		0.33232
P.W. of Total Revenue Requirements:			
Alternate A	876 308		936 277
Alternate B	886 385		948 759
Difference	10 077		12 482
Break-even Capital Cost of Alternate B	586 509		585 192
Difference, $		1317	
Difference, %		0.22	

The procedure is the same as followed in Example I. Comparative results are given in Table 6.1. Alternate A is the economic choice under either discount rate. The present-worth difference between A and B is slightly larger when $r = i - tbB$, and this is reflected in the lower required capital cost of Alternate B for break-even.

DISCOUNTED CASH FLOW METHOD

The Discounted Cash Flow (DCF) method is most often associated with the appraisal of 'opportunity' or 'discretionary' investments in industries other than the electric utility industry. The procedure is the reverse of the Revenue Requirements method. Instead of assuming (or deciding upon) a minimum acceptable return, then calculating required revenues, DCF first estimates revenues, then calculates return. The plan with the highest return is the economic choice. In some problems—investing in increased production capacity, for example—it is possible to estimate increased product sales, in which case these are the revenues used in the DCF method. If the calculated return is sufficient, the investment is made; if not, there may be no investment at all. As noted at the beginning of Chapter 5, this situation does not usually occur in electric utilities. The choice is between alternate facilities, the existence of which will not change the level of electricity production or (directly) of revenues. This situation may also exist in nonutility industry, where the investment may be solely for the purpose of reducing costs at the same production level.

Where there are no actual revenue changes, the DCF method, in effect, treats cost savings as revenues. This is necessary in order to calculate the income tax effect. A reduction of expense has exactly the same effect on income taxes as an increase in revenues. This device may be used to analyze the previous example using the DCF method. In this method, only cash quantities, or 'cash flows,' are considered, expenditures being counted negative and cash received positive. The idea is to list the cash flows during the life of the investment, then, by trial and error, determine the interest rate at which they must be discounted to exactly equal the initial investment. This rate is the Discounted Cash Flow Rate of Return (DCFR), and it is an *after-tax return*.

Example of DCF Method

As with many economic methodologies, there is no unanimity of opinion with respect to the details of the DCF calculation (Abdelsamad, 1973). The following discussion is based on the principles described by Peters (1974).

The DCF method produces the same evaluation as the Revenue Requirements method, if the latter has used a fixed-charge rate leveled at the after-tax discount rate; i.e., $r = i\text{-}tbB$. This will be demonstrated using the break-even results of Example II, given in Table 6.1.

The DCF analysis may be performed by calculating the return to be had by investing in A instead of B. This involves an incremental investment, at break-even, of 600 000 − 585 192, or 14 808. The incremental operating-cost savings are the incentive for this investment.

Method I: Complete Analysis. Two calculational procedures, producing the same result, will be illustrated. The first, shown in Table 6.2, produces income tax, operating, and source-of-funds statements completely consistent with the accounting principles outlined in Chapter 3 if the gross savings are interpreted as incremental gross income, or revenues. The cash flow used in the DCF method is seen to be the familiar 'cash from operations' of the source-of-funds statement, but adjusted for after-tax interest. The rationale for this adjustment will be explained subsequently.

Referring to Table 6.2, line 1 shows the incremental investment in Alternate A as negative, indicating a cash outflow. Lines 2–4 give the operating costs of the original example and the savings of Alternate A over B.

In the income tax statement of lines 5–10, the operating savings are interpreted as gross income. The tax depreciation is SYD for four years [see eqn (3.6)]. The ad valorem tax is 5% of 14 808, and the interest on long-term debt is 10% of half the investment. The taxable income for year 1 is negative, and since we are calculating only the incremental effect of this investment on the total firm, the result is a reduction in income tax; so the tax of 8354 is a positive number, indicating relative cash inflow. This is reversed in years 4 and 5.

The operating statement is straightforward, using book depreciation and other normal deductions from gross income to arrive at reported net income. Note the deferred income tax, which, under normalization, is calculated as the tax rate times the difference between tax and book depreciation.

Lines 19–22 of Table 6.2 represent the portion of the statement of Source and Disposition of Funds that shows cash generated from operations, frequently generically termed 'cash flow.' As described in Chapter 3, it begins with net income, then adds back in those deductions from gross income which did not represent cash payments: in this case, book depreciation and deferred income tax.

The interest adjustment of line 23 is $(1\text{-}t) \times$ (interest), or $0.52 \times 741 = 385$. It is added to correct for the fact that part of the investment was debt-financed. The rate of return calculated in the DCF method is intended to be independent of the method of financing, in the sense that return to equity is the

Table 6.2. DCF calculation.

Line No.		Year 1	Year 2	Year 3	Year 4	Year 5
1	Incr. Investment	− 14 808				
2	Alt. A Op. Costs	60 000	60 000	50 000	25 000	20 000
3	Alt. B Op. Costs	50 000	50 000	50 000	50 000	50 000
4	Operating Savings	− 10 000	− 10 000	0	25 000	30 000
	Income Tax Statement					
5	Gross Income	− 10 000	− 10 000	0	25 000	30 000
6	Tax Depreciation	− 5 923	− 4 442	− 2 962	− 1 480	0
7	Ad Valorem Tax	− 741	− 741	− 741	− 741	− 741
8	Interest	− 741	− 741	− 741	− 741	− 741
9	Taxable Income	− 17 405	− 15 924	− 4 444	22 038	28 518
10	Tax @ 0.48	8 354	7 644	2 133	− 10 578	− 13 689
	Operating Statement					
11	Gross Income	− 10 000	− 10 000	0	25 000	30 000
12	Book Depreciation	− 2 962	− 2 962	− 2 962	− 2 962	− 2 962
13	Ad Valorem Tax	− 741	− 741	− 741	− 741	− 741
14	Income Tax	8 354	7 644	2 133	− 10 578	− 13 689
15	Def. Income Tax	− 1 421	− 710	0	710	1 421
16	Investment Tax Cr.	592				
17	Interest	− 741	− 741	− 741	− 741	− 741
18	Net Income	− 6 919	− 7 510	− 2 311	10 688	13 288
	Source of Funds Statement					
19	Net Income	− 6 919	− 7 510	− 2 311	10 688	13 288
20	Book Depreciation	2 962	2 962	2 962	2 962	2 962
21	Def. Income Tax	1 421	710	0	− 710	− 1 421
22	Cash from Operations	− 2 536	− 3 838	651	12 940	14 829
23	+ Interest Adj.	385	385	385	385	385
24	Cash Flow	− 2 151	− 3 453	1 036	13 325	15 214
25	P.W. @ 9.6% DCF Rate	− 1 963	− 2 875	787	9 235	9 620

Sum of Present Worth of All Years (Discounted Cash Flow) = 14 805

ultimate criterion of the managers of the firm. If debt financing is actually used, it is merely a device by which management operates to optimize return to shareholders.* This is consistent with the concept of 'internal rate of return' or 'after-tax return' implicit in the use of i-tbB as discount rate for leveling the fixed-charge rate in the Revenue Requirements method.

The cash flows of line 24 are discounted at various rates by a trial-and-error method until a rate is found which makes the sum of their present worths equal to the original investment. As Table 6.2 shows, this rate is 9.6%, which is i-tbB, thus demonstrating the equivalence of the DCF and Revenue Requirements method for the break-even example.

*This management philosophy may not be as freely exercised in regulated electric utilities as it is in nonregulated industries, where the DCF method is primarily used.

Method II: Short Analysis. Examination of Table 6.2 will reveal that the interest adjustment of line 23 effectively eliminates consideration of interest, and that both book depreciation and deferred taxes are superfluous components because they are first subtracted from gross income, then added back in to obtain cash flow. Again, this is consistent with the after-tax philosophy of discount rate for the Revenue Requirements method. These items do not appear in the fixed-charge rate of eqn (5.44).

Accordingly, there is no need to go through all of the steps of Table 6.2 except, as here, to illuminate the theory. The usual practice is illustrated in Table 6.3. The taxable income is calculated ignoring interest on debt. The 'net income' is what is left from taxable income after paying taxes. To obtain cash flow, tax depreciation is added back in because that is what was deducted in obtaining net income. The cash flows of line 9 are identical to those of line 24 of Table 6.2, and, of course, the DCF rate of return is also the same.

This is a beautifully simple procedure, innocent of the complications of book depreciation method, tax deferrals, and, seemingly, method of financing. The calculation is made *as though* the financing were to be 100% equity, but no such assumption is necessary to the validity of the method. It is only necessary to bear in mind that the DCF rate of return (DCFR) equals i-tbB. Return to equity, r_1, may be calculated as follows:

$$DCFR = i\text{-}tbB; \tag{6.1}$$

$$i = bB + (1 - B)r_1. \tag{6.2}$$

Substituting,

$$r_1 = [DCFR - (1 - t)bB]/(1 - B). \tag{6.3}$$

The interpretation of the DCF result is that, since the additional investment in Alternate A produces exactly 9.6% discounted rate of return as compared to Alternate B, there is no choice between them; and this is the same conclusion

Table 6.3. Simplified DCF calculation.

Line No.		Year 1	Year 2	Year 3	Year 4	Year 5
1	Gross Income	− 10 000	− 10 000	0	25 000	30 000
2	Tax Depreciation	− 5 923	− 4 442	− 2 962	− 1 480	0
3	Ad Valorem Tax	− 741	− 741	− 741	− 741	− 741
4	Taxable Income	− 16 664	− 15 183	− 3 703	22 779	29 259
5	Tax @ 0.48	7 998	7 288	1 777	− 10 934	− 14 045
6	Investment Tax Cr.	592				
7	Net Income	− 8 074	− 7 895	− 1 926	11 845	15 214
8	Tax Depreciation	5 923	4 442	2 962	1 480	0
9	Cash Flow	− 2 151	− 3 453	1 036	13 325	15 214
	DCFR = 9.6%					

that is reached using the Revenue Requirements method. This example was, of course, designed to demonstrate the comparability of the two methods. In the usual use of DCF, alternate plans would be judged by their rates of return, the highest one indicating the economic choice, but only if it were equal to or greater than $i\text{-}tbB$, the desired minimum internal rate of return.

OTHER METHODS

Net Present Worth Method

The Net Present Worth method requires the calculation of positive and negative cash flows, as in the DCF method; but instead of solving for the DCFR, a desired rate of return is used to calculate the present worth of all cash flows. In the previous example, the cash flows for each alternate (instead of for the incremental investment) would be set down in tables similar to Table 6.3, and the present worth calculated, including the initial investment. The alternate with the largest net present worth is the economic choice. If the internal rate of return, $i\text{-}tbB$, were chosen as the desired return, the net present worths of Alternates A and B in the preceding example would be equal.

Payout Method

To illustrate the Payout Method, the incremental investment device of the DCF example must again be used. Line 1 of Table 6.3 gives the incremental cash flows that are conceived as 'returning' the investment as follows:

Year	Investment Cash Flow	Cash Flow Benefits	Cumulative Total Cash Flow
1	− 14 808	− 10 000	− 24 808
2		− 10 000	− 34 808
3		0	− 34 808
4		25 000	− 9 808
5		30 000	20 192

In this case, the investment is said to be 'paid out' in somewhat more than four years, the time at which the cumulative cash flow becomes positive. This is the 'Gross Payout' method. The 'Net Payout' method is identical in procedure, but uses the net cash flow of line 9, Table 6.3, giving a slightly different payout time in this example.

The Payout method is not, and should not be considered, a method of economic comparison because it ignores the time value of money. In nonregulated industries, however, it is sometimes used as a preliminary means for ranking projects of equal lives, to be followed by DCF or Net Present Worth analyses for actual decision.

CHOICE OF METHOD

The choice among the three described methods (Revenue Requirements, DCF, and Net Present Worth) may be based upon practice, ease of calculation, and economic validity. All three, consistently implemented, will produce correct results. The Revenue Requirements method appears simpler from a calculational viewpoint. The fixed-charge-rate calculation is admittedly complex; but once a value is calculated for a given set of conditions, it may be used for any number of similar problems. Both the DCF and Net Present Worth methods require tabular calculations which are repeated for each case; and the former requires an iterative procedure as well.

In electric utility practice, the Revenue Requirements method is almost universal. This has come about, probably, because the method is parallel in concept to the procedures used by regulatory commissions in establishing allowable revenues for rate-making purposes: (1) establish an allowable rate of return; (2) apply this rate to the investment, or rate base; (3) add allowable expenses for taxes and operations and obtain total allowable revenue.

For these reasons, the Revenue Requirements method will be used exclusively in the remainder of this book.

7
Electric Utility System Loads

Some knowledge of the load characteristics of an electric utility is essential to a generation economic analysis. These characteristics are determined by the living habits and operating patterns of the individuals and organizations who use electric power. Such habits and patterns are, in turn, a function of the particular society involved, modified by many other factors, including the state of economic development and the climate. Thus, there can be considerable variation in load characteristics from country to country, and from area to area within one country.

In common usage, the terminology of electric power systems is, unfortunately, neither precise nor always accurate. The engineer knows that *power* is the rate of doing work, or of producing *energy,* and that power is measured in kW and energy in kWh. But the terms *load* and *demand,* although perhaps clearly defined in some cases, are not always used consistently. A *load* curve, for example, defines power as a function of time—hence for a given period, it also defines energy. Similarly, 'demand' may be used in reference to either power or energy. In this book, both 'load' and 'demand' will be used to mean power, unless modified by the word 'energy.'

Two other terms about which there is frequently some confusion are 'load factor' and 'capacity factor.' Load factor is the ratio of the load energy over a period of time to the energy which would have been consumed had the power remained constant at its peak value for the entire period. It may also be thought of as the average power divided by the peak power.

The definition of capacity factor is similar to that of load factor, but it pertains to the output of individual generating units, not to load. Capacity factor is the ratio of energy generated by a unit over a period of time to the energy which would have been generated had it operated continuously at its maximum capability during the period.

SYSTEM LOAD COMPONENTS

Generating capacity is installed in response to a need to supply a peak demand for power. If there is sufficient generation reliably to meet the peak power demand, there will be no difficulty in supplying the energy demand. So generation economic analysis is concerned first with the shape of daily, seasonal, and annual load power curves. And, in general, these data are available because utilities record hourly loads for the system as a whole.

This breakdown of system loads into components defined by time interval is the first categorization of load. The second is into components defined by class of user, the most usual being residential or domestic, heavy industrial, and light industrial or commercial. Because each of these user classes generally is charged for electricity under a different rate schedule, utilities automatically have records of energy usage, by user class, over the billing period, which may be a month or more. But most utilities do not routinely or continually record hourly power demand by user class, although periodic measurements may be taken as an aid to predicting future total system load, or the load on major substations or transmission lines.

The daily, seasonal, and annual load curves result from the independent actions of these various classes of power users, and it will be useful to consider them in the process of developing total system load curves. Historically, electricity was first used for lighting; and this use still tends to dominate the residential portion of the load, depending upon the level of economic development of the area involved. Lighting loads, of course, predominate in the early evening hours and in the winter season, when days are shortest. Other residential applications of electricity—appliances, air-conditioning, electric space heating—make their own unique contributions to the daily and seasonal load curve. For example, in areas of high saturation of television, it is not unusual to find a sharp load peak on Sunday evening during the prime viewing hours—a peak which does not occur at this time on any other day of the week.

Industrial and commercial loads are predominantly daytime loads. Their contribution to the total system load is seen in the generally lower level of weekend and holiday loads in contrast to weekday loads. It is sometimes possible to see a sharp drop in daily load during the noontime shutdown of factories.

Hourly Load Curves

Hourly load curves for summer and winter days are shown in Figs. 7.1 and 7.2. These curves are taken from a large metropolitan system whose air-conditioning saturation is such that its annual peak occurs in the summertime. The peak of the summer-day curve is relatively flat, with loads very close to the daily peak for several hours, indicating the constant effect of air-conditioning load during the warmest portion of the day. By contrast, the winter-day curve has a single sharp peak, which occurs at the coincidence of the residential cooking and lighting loads with the last hour of the industrial and electric railway peaks.

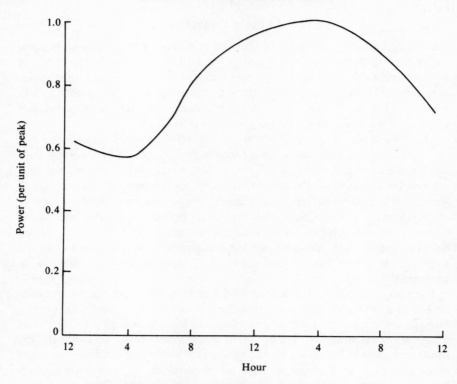

Fig. 7.1. Hourly load curve: summer day.

Three aspects of these hourly load curves are significant with respect to power generation economics. First, the mere fact of a load factor less than unity implies less-than-complete utilization of the capital investment in generating capacity, which must at least equal the peak load. Second, the variability of the hourly loads from a minimum of about 60% to the 100% peak makes it necessary to operate some portion of the connected generation at less than its rating some of the time. This results in poorer fuel economy because the efficiency of generating units is generally lower at part load than at full load. Third, the very rapid rate of increase of load in the morning hours can result in inefficient commitment (connection to the grid) of excess generation in advance, in order to provide adequate ability to follow the load.

The daily load factor varies considerably, depending upon the characteristics of the load area, the season, and whether the day is a weekday or a weekend day. For the system from which these curves are taken, the daily load factor ranged from 0.8 to 0.9. The average of all the days in the year was 0.85.

This average daily load factor will be the basis for synthesizing the total annual load factor; and in the process, some insight will be gained as to those things which influence load shapes and load factors. Let the average daily load factor be designated LF_d. Then,

$$LF_d = 0.85.$$

Each day's load factor is based on its own peak load. The annual load factor is based on the annual peak load. So the relationship of the daily peaks to the annual peak must be considered. This will be done in two steps: first the ratio of daily peaks to monthly peak, then the ratio of monthly peaks to annual peak.

Daily Peak Variations

If the daily peaks within a month are examined, one weekday will be the maximum, hence the peak for the month. Sometimes a pattern of variation of weekday peaks may be recognized (e.g., higher peaks in the early part of the week, when domestic laundry appliances are heavily used); in other cases the day of peak load is determined by random events, such as weather. For the example utility used here, weekday peaks ranged as low as 70% of the monthly peak, while holiday and weekend day peaks dropped to about 40%. These ranges were not the same for all months of the year, but the averages were similar; so for this synthetic example, a simple ratio of average daily peak, PL_d, to monthly peak, PL_m, will be used:

$$PL_d/PL_m = 0.87.$$

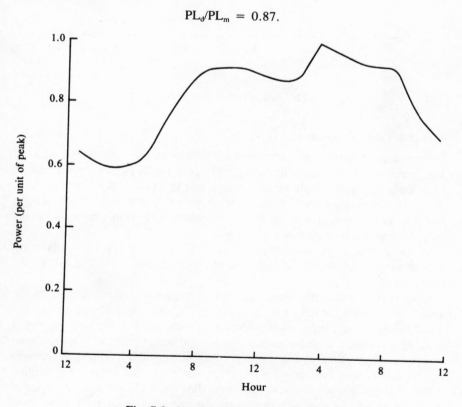

Fig. 7.2. Hourly load curve: winter day.

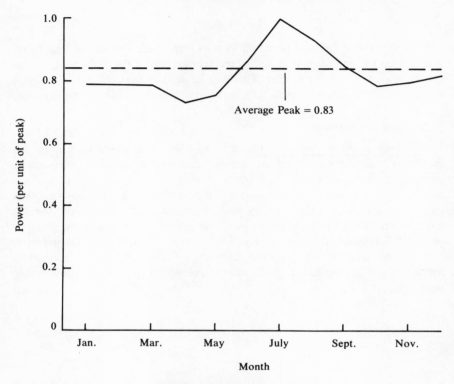

Fig. 7.3. Monthly peak loads.

Monthly Peak Variations

To complete the picture of system loads, it is necessary to consider the seasonal load variations as expressed by the monthly peak loads. Figure 7.3 is a plot of such loads for the example system, which had its peak in the month of July. There is a tremendous variation in the shape of curves such as this among different utility systems. In very warm climates, with high saturation of air-conditioning, the average can be as low as 0.71.

A similar low average will obtain in cool climates with low air-conditioning saturation, but of course in this case the peak month would occur in the wintertime.

Historically, nearly all systems had low average monthly peaks but with the peak load occurring in the winter because lighting use was predominant. As air-conditioning became more widely adopted in some areas, some systems passed through a transition period when the summer and winter peaks were nearly equal and the average monthly peak load was of the order of 0.95. Subsequent growth of air-conditioning then produced the summer peak load curve with varying ratios of summer to winter peak load depending upon climate and saturation of air-conditioning. In one area, however, the combination of rapid population growth and associated home building, coupled with mild winter weather and low power costs, resulted in a growth of residential and commercial electric space-heating load sufficient to more than offset growing air-conditioning load; so that the predominance of the winter peak load over the summer peak remained, despite very high air-conditioning saturation.

ANNUAL LOAD FACTOR: LOAD MANAGEMENT

The average of the monthly peak loads, PL_m, given in Fig. 7.3, expressed in per unit of the annual peak PL_a, is:

$$PL_m/PL_a = 0.83.$$

The annual load factor may now be calculated as:

$$LF_a = LF_d \times \frac{PL_d}{PL_m} \times \frac{PL_m}{PL_a}; \qquad (7.1)$$

thus,

$$LF_a = 0.85 \times 0.87 \times 0.83 = 0.614,$$

which is quite close to the actual load factor of the example utility. Equation (7.1) is not intended to be precise. It was developed as a vehicle for describing load characteristics and, more importantly, to show the possibilities and limitations of load modification, or load management.

The term 'load management' refers to any means by which load curves may be made more nearly flat in shape, i.e. by which the load factor may be increased. In principle, this could be accomplished by automatic time-control of utilization equipment or by incentive pricing of electric energy to induce users to restrict power consumption during periods of anticipated peak loads. The ostensible benefits are greater utilization of generating equipment (hence lower capital investment for a given level of energy production) and less need to generate energy with high fuel costs peaking generation (because peaks would be reduced). One study (Jordan, Marsh, Moisan, and Oplinger, 1976) has suggested that higher load factors may not always be beneficial; but it is also of interest to consider the extent to which annual load factor might be increased.

Referring to Fig. 7.1, if the daily load curves could all be made perfectly flat by load management techniques, LF_d would become unity, and

$$LF_a = 1.0 \times 0.87 \times 0.83 = 0.722.$$

Alternatively, if monthly or seasonal load patterns could be changed, the ratio of monthly average peaks to annual peak might become unity, and

$$LF_a = 0.85 \times 0.87 \times 1.0 = 0.74.$$

The third possible illustration, that of uniform daily peak loads within the month, is not given because voluntary or involuntary control measures to achieve such leveling are more difficult to conceive than those required for daily or seasonal load shaping. The diurnal patterns of electricity use tend to be similar for all users of a particular class, and it may, therefore, be possible to adjust the daily load shape by incentive rates, perhaps facilitated by user-supplied energy storage devices. Similarly, seasonal usage may be controllable by incentive rates. Short of a major social revolution, however, it will not be possible to produce Saturday, Sunday, and holiday peak loads equal to workday peak loads; and even the variations in the latter are probably uncontrollable because of the random nature of their causes and the diversity of individual social and economic habits.

The discussion thus far has considered load factor as an aggregate characteristic of electricity users—as 'seen' at the meters of the supplying utility system. If individual users find it desirable to invest in storage devices to change their own load factors, this will produce a change in the utility's load factor as seen at the meter. On the other hand, if the utility itself invests in storage equipment, there will be a change in its *apparent* load factor—as seen by the power output of generating units—but no change in the underlying *utilization* load factor. The difference, of course, is the matter of who makes the investment in the storage devices; and any economic analysis of load management should recognize this. Further, it is important when comparing load factors among utility systems to be sure that they are all referenced so as to exclude the effect of storage owned or operated by the utilities.

The load factor of the Central Electricity Generating Board of Great Britain for the year 1975–76 was about 57%. The average of United States systems for the year 1976 was 62.6%, but the range of load factor among even the large, component U.S. systems was from 70% to 47%. Some smaller systems, serving areas of low population and power density, predominantly rural areas, may have load factors as low as 35%. It is not always realistic to assume that such systems may be economically integrated with others to obtain the benefits of diversification and resulting higher load factors because distances may be so great or terrain so difficult as to preclude the required transmission facilities. It is necessary, therefore, to give consideration to the economic design of generation systems for low load factors as well as for moderate and high load factors.

LOAD DURATION CURVE

A final load curve which will be useful later in considering the application of generation is the load duration curve, giving a picture of an entire year's load. This is shown in Fig. 7.4. It may be thought of as the assembly of all of the hourly loads in the year (8760 for a non–leap year) in descending order of magnitude. This curve is not chronological, but its load factor may be determined in the same way as the curve of hourly loads for a single day, i.e. the ratio of the actual kilowatt hours represented by the area under the curve to the peak load for the year multiplied by 8760.

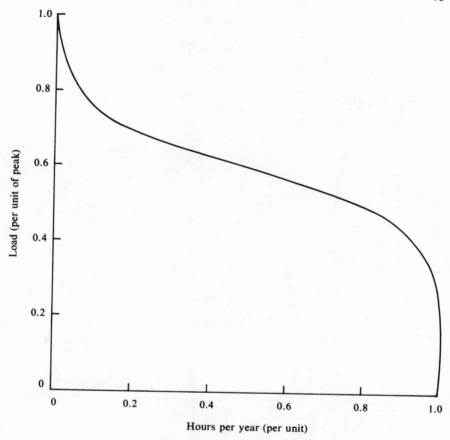

Fig. 7.4. Load duration curve.

GROWTH OF LOADS

Occasionally a power system that has been purchasing all of its electric power will decide to do its own generation, in which case there is an opportunity to design and build, at one time, a complete system of generating units to supply an existing total load. But this situation is rare, and the more common problem is to select generation to augment an existing system in anticipation of future load growth. The first consideration is to provide sufficient generating capacity (power). This is usually related to the annual peak load, because utility system loads tend to be cyclical on an annual basis, and because this is a natural planning period for most people. Energy growth, as contrasted to peak load growth, is probably a more fundamental characteristic of power system loads, and it is, hence, more easily predicted, but its effect on the required amount of generating capacity is indirect, and it is ultimately necessary to predict the future peak load.

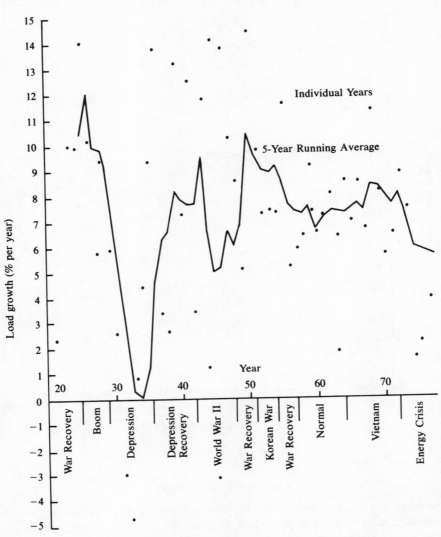

Fig. 7.5. Annual peak load growth; U.S. utilities.

The growth in electric utility loads is the result of several underlying factors of long-term significance coupled with the shorter-term effects of economic and weather cycles. The first long-term growth factor is population. Added to this is the increase in penetration of common electric-utilization equipment, whether domestic or industrial. The development of new electrical technology may also increase energy usage per capita, for example, television, electric furnaces, and aluminum reduction. Finally, there may be increased growth effects from the substitution of electric energy for fossil fuels as a result of changing price relationships or shortages.

Forecasting the effects of all of these factors on future energy use and then translating the results into future peak loads is a very specialized and difficult art. Figure 7.5 shows the year-to-year and five-year cumulative average growth in peak load of the United States electric utility industry, calculated from data published by the Edison Electric Institute. Considering that individual systems have even greater variations than shown here, it is not surprising that even with the best load forecasting it is necessary to consider the uncertainty of load forecasts when planning for future generation.

8
System Operation

As noted previously, generation economic analysis implies a projection, or prediction, of the economic results of operating a given generation system under an assumed choice of future generation facilities to serve a postulated future load. Fundamentally, then, the analysis is a simulation of future system operation, either real or inferred. Even in the simple direct-unit analysis of the generation cost of a single unit, the selection of a capacity factor for the calculation infers the future operation of the unit within the framework of the total generation system. Whether the analysis method is thus one of inference of future operation or of actual simulation, a knowledge of system operating principles is essential if credible results are to be obtained. In this chapter, a brief review of those principles will be given.

OPERATION FOR RELIABILITY

The first objective of a generation system is to secure reliability, by which is meant continuous electricity supply within an acceptably small range of voltage and frequency variation. In essence, this requires precisely matching the output of the generation system to the load, a process which embraces consideration of load and generation variations within time periods ranging from less than a second to several years. At the short end of this range are normal load changes and generation changes resulting from sudden failure of units. At the long end are the normal growth of load and the construction period of large units. The long-time provision of installed capacity adequate to match anticipated load growth may be called capacity or reserve *planning,* a subject which will be discussed in the next chapter. *Operation* considers only time periods of up to a year.

Because of the uncertainty of both capacity availability and loads, an essential part of operation for reliability is the establishment of reserve capacity in various time frames.

Seasonal Reserve: Maintenance

Reserve is the difference between capacity and load. When expressed as a percentage, the base is ordinarily the load. *Installed reserve* is normally thought of as the difference between the installed capacity and the peak load for a particular year. As such, it is a rough measure of the potential operating reliability of the system for the year. Consideration of the seasonal variation of loads, however, reveals that reserve margin, hence reliability, varies throughout the year from a minimum at the time of peak load to a maximum at the lowest seasonal load. This variation is important in scheduling the maintenance of generating units.

Unit Maintenance Requirements. All generating units must be removed from service periodically for predictable routine inspection or overhaul, the duration of which varies with the type of unit and, to a lesser extent, its accumulated operating time. Pressure vessels used in steam plants require safety inspections, typically annually. Rotating machinery may be scheduled for disassembly and preventive maintenance inspection on a two- or three-year cycle. The combustion components of steam generators and gas turbines require regular cleaning and replacement of parts. Nuclear reactors must be shut down at predictable intervals for refueling. Hydroelectric units require down-time for dam and penstock inspections, and for repair of damage from erosion.

The percentage of the time that a unit is unavailable for service because of planned maintenance or refueling is called its *planned outage rate*. The typical range of such rates is from 2% or less for hydroelectric units to 12% or more for large coal-fired steam units.

System Maintenance Scheduling. The prime objective of maintenance scheduling is to minimize the risk of insufficient capacity throughout the year. Figure 8.1 is a plot of a typical monthly peak load profile, showing the 'load-drop' area below the annual peak load of 1000 MW. An installed reserve of 20% gives installed capacity of 1200 MW. If we assume that the average of the monthly peak loads is 850 MW, the load-drop area may be calculated as $12(1000 - 850) = 1800$ MW-months. If it is further assumed that the average planned outage rate of the system generation is 10%, the total required annual maintenance is $0.1(12)(1200) = 1440$ MW-months. Since the required maintenance is less than the load-drop area, maintenance can be fitted in without requiring any units to be out of service during the month of peak load. This in turn means that the *available reserve* each month will be no less than the installed reserve of 20% for the year.

If, on the other hand, the shape of the monthly peak load curve were such as to give less than 1440 MW-months of load-drop, there would be some time during the year when the sum of monthly peak load plus capacity on scheduled maintenance would be greater than the load alone in the peak month. This would produce an available reserve, in that month, less than the installed reserve. If

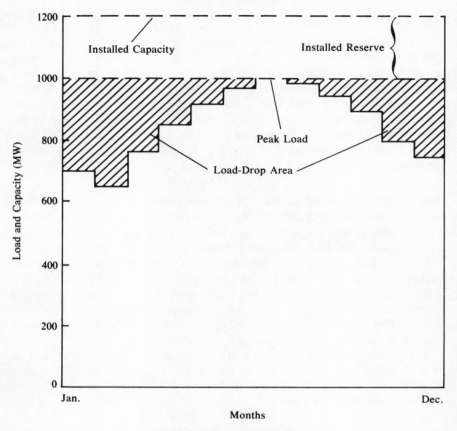

Fig. 8.1. Monthly load profile.

a reserve margin of 20% were considered essential for adequate reliability, it would be necessary to install more capacity to bring the available reserve back up to 20%.

Regardless of whether additional installed reserve is required because of maintenance needs, the scheduling of maintenance will ordinarily be done so as to level the risk of insufficient capacity throughout the year, and this tends to maximize the annual reliability. Garver (1972) developed a simple and effective method of accomplishing this using the concept of effective capacity (see Chapter 9).

Daily Operating Reserve

The subject of operating reserve has to do with how the operator of a generation system (the dispatcher) disposes the available reserves each day to match the varying load and to provide for contingencies. Operating reserve is the difference between the anticipated load and the generating capacity which can produce output within a time period short enough to maintain acceptable frequency under credible operating contingencies. Total operating reserve is made up of components designated for each contingency. Terminology and practice in this field vary considerably, but the following discussion will serve to identify principles and typical operating practice.

Spinning Reserve. For each day's operations, there has been prepared beforehand a forecast of the hourly loads. Because some of the units have been shut down overnight to save fuel, the first consideration is a schedule for restarting and synchronizing units to prepare for the rapid morning-load buildup. This schedule of units to be started is called a 'commitment list,' and it is ordinarily arranged in order of increasing unit fuel cost of generation. Because the rate of load increase may be much greater than the rate at which units can be started and synchronized, units are started well in advance of load requirement, which results in relatively high (50% to 100%) excess capacity during the period of rapid load increase. This excess is called 'spinning reserve' because it represents units which are synchronized and operating at less than maximum capability.

Spinning reserve is costly because units operating at part load are less efficient than when at or near their full-load points; hence the total capacity to be committed for the day is calculated to exceed the forecast peak load by a minimum acceptable amount, usually in the range from 4% to 8%. This amount of spinning reserve is necessary to provide for load forecast error, frequency regulation, and dynamic pickup, as described in the following paragraphs.

Although daily load forecasting is a highly developed art, there is always the possibility of underestimation. A spinning reserve allowance of 1% to 2% for load forecast error is typical, with the requirement that it be available in one or two minutes.

Even if the capacity on the line were exactly equal to the maximum load, there would still be a requirement for excess capacity to permit rapid enough response to small load increases to avoid excessive frequency excursions. This regulation function also typically requires 1% to 2% spinning reserve; but it must be available within a response time of two to five seconds.

Finally, there must be a component of spinning reserve for the dynamic pickup of load dropped by the sudden loss of a loaded generating unit. If only such hazards associated with a single system, ignoring interconnections, are considered, the required amount of dynamic pickup capacity would ordinarily be equal to the output of the largest unit; and this might represent 10% or more of the peak load. With adequately interconnected systems, however, each system need only provide dynamic pickup corresponding to the ratio of its capacity to the total effective interconnected capacity. This may reduce any one system's spinning reserve for dynamic pickup to the range of 2% to 4%. In order to avoid excessive frequency swings and the risk of instability, this capacity should have a response of five to ten seconds.

Nonspinning Reserve. After a sudden loss of generation in one part of a pool or interconnected system has been made up by the spinning reserves of the total capacity, power flows on transmission lines will be distorted from their normal schedules, with the possibility that some lines will be thermally overloaded. If such is the case, it is necessary to have some generation available in the deficient area to restore these lines to their normal loadings before conductor damage occurs—perhaps in five to ten minutes. This thermal backup requirement may vary from zero to 10%.

It also may be desirable to have up to 10% reserve available in from five to thirty minutes as contingency backup—to reestablish dynamic-pickup spinning reserve in preparation for the event of a second sudden loss of generation.

Because these last two categories of reserve have response requirements which are within the range of starting times of some kinds of generation, it may be considered unnecessary to cover them with actual, synchronized spinning capacity if fast-start types of generation are a part of the system. They may thus sometimes be referred to as nonspinning reserve.

Another alleviation of generation deficiency which is not reserve generation capacity but which is frequently included in the category of nonspinning reserve is interruptible load. Certain industrial power users may operate under a lower-than-normal rate schedule which allows the utility to interrupt service after a specified time of notification. The utility may use such agreements to cover the categories of operating reserve falling outside the notification time.

Table 8.1 summarizes the categories of operating reserve with typical quantities and response times for each. It should be noted again that the terminology is not universal, and that reserve values and response times for operating utilities will vary widely as necessary to fit individual conditions.

Unit Operating Characteristics

The system operating requirements discussed above are generally attainable using available kinds of generating units. In most cases, however, it is necessary to distribute the duty among several units in order to achieve sufficiently rapid aggregate load response. And because generating units of various kinds have different inherent or designed-in capabilities, it is important to recognize system operating needs when comparing alternate generating facilities. As with system

Table 8.1. Operating reserve components.

Component	Percent of Load	Response Time
Daily-Load Forecast Error	1– 2	1– 2 min.
Regulation	1– 2	2– 5 sec.
Dynamic Pickup	2– 4	5–10 sec.
Thermal Backup	0–10	5–10 min.
Contingency Backup	0–10	5–30 min.

Table 8.2. Dynamic characteristics of generating units.

| Generation Type | Emergency Fast Pickup | | Maximum Rate for Sustained Load Changes | Starting Time |
	Amount Available % of Rating	Time Required		
Fossil-Steam				
Gas or Oil	20	10 sec.	2–5%/min.	Hours
	30	30 sec.		
Coal	15	10 sec.	2–5%/min.	Hours
	20	30 sec.		
Nuclear Steam	8	10 sec.	1½–3%/min.	Hours
	20	30 sec.		
Gas Turbine				
Heavy-Duty	100	5 sec.	20%/sec.	3–10 min.
Aircraft-Derivative	100	5 sec.	20%/sec.	1–5 min.
Hydro				
High Head	0	10 sec.	1%/sec.	1–5 min.
Medium Head	20	10 sec.	5%/sec.	3–5 min.
Low Head	100	10 sec.	10%/sec.	1–5 min.

operating requirements, it is not possible precisely to define generating-unit operating characteristics, but the following discussion will identify typical ranges and some of the reasons therefor.

Starting and Loading Rates. Table 8.2 gives representative values of starting and loading times for thermal and hydroelectric generating units (Tice, 1967). The starting time is the period required for combustion, raising pressure and temperature, accelerating to speed, and synchronizing. The emergency fast-pickup values are generally based on the inherent limits of thermal and mechanical time constants, and assume modern design and provision for special forcing signals (which are not always applied). In particular, the values for fossil-steam units imply well-controlled boilers and fuel systems.

Nuclear unit characteristics vary widely with type of reactor and the state of design maturity. The values shown are typical of light-water-moderated-and-cooled reactors.

The data given for gas turbines apply to simple-cycle, single-shaft units where load response is limited only by the permissible rate of temperature change and the resulting thermal stress. Infrequent emergency load change may be very rapid, although normal load changes should be very much slower if excessive maintenance is to be avoided. Starting times shown are also minimum and pertain to emergency conditions.

The load response of high-head hydroelectric plants is zero (it may even be negative) for the first few seconds. The load change rate of hydro units is largely a function of the time required safely to accelerate the water filling the penstock.

Loading Limits. Minimum loading limits may be imposed on generating units by physical or economic considerations. Some boilers of the once-through type may require a fairly large minimum flow of water and steam to prevent hot spots and subsequent tube failure. In pulverized-coal-fired boilers particularly, the requirement of stable combustion conditions in the furnace imposes a high minimum load. While this condition can be alleviated by an admixture of oil fuel at light loads, the result is an economic penalty if oil is more costly than coal. Depending on the type of coal and the furnace design, the control of slagging may dictate a minimum practical operating output.

The existence of conditions such as the above may result in minimum loads as high as 50% of rating. In their absence, 10% is a practical minimum to maintain stable control and avoid reverse power flow in the event of system frequency swings. Nuclear, gas turbine, and hydro units can normally operate satisfactorily at as low as 10% to 25% of rating. Pumped-storage hydro units are an exception, since in the pumping mode, they usually must operate near full load.

Overload capability of generating units may be obtained in steam units by over-pressure, and by removing feedwater heaters from service, thus allowing more steam flow through the lower pressure stages of the turbine. Similarly, gas turbines may be operated above rated temperature, and hydro units at greater than rated head. Such overloads, however, may infringe upon the design margins of boilers, turbines, and generators, and are deprecated except in infrequent emergencies where the risk is known and acceptable.

Energy Source Limits. Generating units using fossil or nuclear fuel generally have an inventory of fuel at the plant site which is adequate for at least 60 to 90 days of full-load operation. Their energy sources may thus be considered unlimited from the viewpoint of normal system operation. Many conventional hydro units have days or weeks of storage as an inherent part of the hydraulic system, and this is adequate for the purpose of insuring reliable operation of the power system under contingency conditions.

This is not necessarily the case with other types of generation. Pumped-storage hydro units may have limited energy capability because of the economic limits on the size of the upper reservoir. Some installations have been built with as little as five hours of storage. There is a real concern as to whether such a plant can be considered a reliable source of power under emergency conditions, when it might be required to operate on peak for three or four days with limited opportunity to recharge the storage reservoir.

Solar and wind-power plants, though not currently in wide use, may in the future find a degree of application in electric utility systems. The limited, random, and unpredictable nature of their energy sources almost certainly precludes their receiving full credit as reliable capacity, even on a long-term basis. Obviously, such plants will receive no consideration as part of daily operating reserve.

OPERATION FOR ECONOMY

The first objective of system operation is to serve the load reliably. The second is to do so at minimum cost. Minimum cost means *minimum total system cost,* i.e. the cost that will ultimately determine required revenue and appear on the income statement determining net income for the year. No consideration is given to whether a particular unit or group of units is operating at *its* lowest cost. The only costs that can be controlled at the time of operating decision are those for fuel and, to a lesser degree, operating labor and materials, and maintenance labor and materials. Capital costs are 'sunk' costs and hence cannot be influenced by operating decisions.

In operating a generating system for maximum economy, the dispatcher must first select, from the units that are available to him during the load period under consideration, those that can combine to produce lowest cost. He then prepares a time schedule for starting and stopping each unit. The process of starting and synchronizing a unit so that it is ready to assume load is called 'commitment.' The second step is to distribute the required total output for each hour (or shorter time period) among the committed units so as to produce minimum total cost. This process is called 'economic dispatch.'

Daily Commitment of Units

A commitment list is a list of available units arranged in order of starting priority, or 'merit order.' In theory, the order of starting should be that which will produce the lowest cost of system operation considering future dispatch over a period of several daily load cycles. This criterion is not often used literally, however, because it would require continuous simulation calculations which are not considered warranted by the relatively small potential cost savings. Instead, a common practice is to establish the list in order of total fuel and maintenance cost per kWh at the full-load point for each unit.

In the actual commitment process, such a priority list is the basic guide for the dispatcher, but it may be modified by additional considerations relating to the peculiar characteristics of individual generating units. Common are start-up and shutdown rules. Such rules say, in effect, 'Do not start Unit A unless the load will be such as to require that it be committed for at least four hours,' and similarly for shutdown rules. These rules are a recognition of two things: (1) that the amount of fuel consumed in starting a unit may be greater than that which would be saved if that unit were operated instead of the next unit in the priority order; (2) that there are hazards associated with starting and stopping a large and complex generating unit, and the risk of failure or of increased maintenance cost may not be worth the fuel savings.

One of the results of commitment rules is excess spinning reserve during much of the daily load cycle: commitment cannot follow the sum of load and minimum required spinning reserve as closely as would be desirable for the lowest fuel consumption. In practice, there may be only three or four periods of constant commitment during the day.

Economic Dispatch

For each period of constant commitment, it is necessary to distribute load among units in the most economic manner. For a given system electrical output, it is desired to minimize the cost of fuel input and of incurred maintenance expense. The principle of equal incremental costs is most commonly used for this purpose. It may be implemented by tables or curves of incremental costs, by loading slide rules, or by computer systems which not only continuously compute economic loadings, but may also automatically adjust unit outputs for maximum economy.

Thermal Unit Dispatch. Figure 8.2 shows thermal characteristics typical of a conventional boiler and steam turbine-generator. In the upper graph of Fig. 8.2, the input would be measured in Btu/hr or kJ/hr, the output in kW. Heat rate is defined as the ratio of input to output, which in absolute units is Btu/kWh or kJ/kWh. In the upper graph of Fig. 8.2, the heat rate is thus the slope of a ray from the origin to any load point on the input-output curve. The slope of the ray marked A gives a heat rate at the full-load (1.0 per unit) point of 1.0 per unit (p.u.). Ray B has a slope of $0.33/0.25 = 1.32$ p.u., which means that the heat rate at 0.25 p.u. output is 1.32 times the full-load heat rate. The lower graph of Fig. 8.2 gives the *total heat rate* curve over the rest of the load range. At zero output, the heat rate is, of course, infinite because of the input required to overcome windage, friction, and auxiliary power losses.

The *incremental heat rate* is defined as the slope of a tangent to the input-output curve at any particular load point. At 0.25 p.u. output, the tangent at Point C has a slope of about 0.85, which is plotted on the lower graph of Fig. 8.2. Once a unit has been committed, its no-load heat input, measured at the intercept of the input-output curve at the input axis, may be considered in the nature of a 'sunk cost' for so long as the unit is on the line. The decision to load or not to load the unit is therefore made solely on the basis of its incremental heat rate in comparison with the incremental heat rates of other units which are on the line at the same time. *The theory of economic loading states that minimum total system input is obtained when units are operated at equal incremental rates.*

The 'incremental rates' to be used are not simply the incremental heat rates as developed in Fig. 8.2, for not all units may use fuel of the same price, and it is cost input, not merely heat input, that is to be minimized. Further, it may be possible to recognize differences in incremental maintenance cost among units, and in this case the incremental rates include these costs as well. The total incremental rate as used for economic loading purposes is frequently designated by the symbol λ.

To illustrate the use of incremental rates, a set of unit loading curves will be developed using a system of five generating units identified by the letters A through E, with characteristics as given in Table 8.3, and aggregate capacity of 1450 MW. Figure 8.3 is a plot of the incremental rate of each unit over its

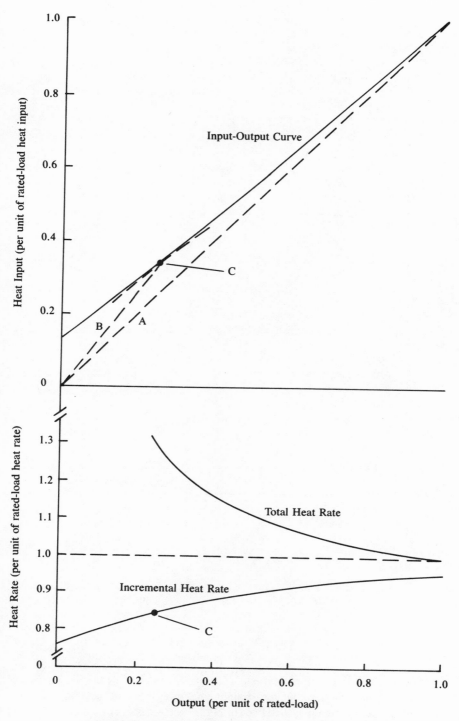

Fig. 8.2. Input-output and heat-rate characteristics.

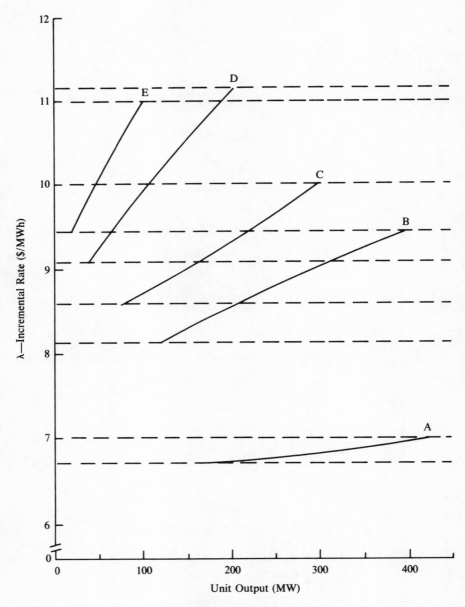

Fig. 8.3. Incremental rates.

load range. (Actual incremental-rate characteristics have significant curvature and even discontinuities, but the straight lines used here are adequate for this example.) The horizontal dashed lines of Fig. 8.3 are lines of constant incremental rate drawn at break-points of the loading schedule. The object is to determine

Table 8.3. Unit cost characteristics.

			Units		
	A	B	C	D	E
Full Load, MW	450	400	300	200	100
Heat Rate, kJ/kWh	10 000	9 500	10 000	10 500	11 000
(Btu/kWh)	(9 479)	(9 005)	(9 479)	(9 953)	(10 427)
Fuel Cost, $/GJ	0.70	100	100	100	100
($/MBtu)	(0.74)	(1.06)	(1.06)	(1.06)	(1.06)
Minimum Load, MW	150	120	75	40	20
IHR* @ min. load, kJ/kWh	9 570	8 150	8 600	9 100	9 450
(Btu/kWh)	(9 071)	(7 725)	(8 152)	(8 626)	(8 957)
IHR @ full load, kJ/kWh	10 000	9 450	10 000	11 100	11 000
(Btu/kWh)	(9 479)	(8 957)	(9 479)	(10 521)	(10 427)
λ @ min. load, $/MWh	6.7	8.15	8.6	9.1	9.45
λ @ full load, $/MWh	7.0	9.45	10.0	11.1	11.0

* Incremental Heat Rate

how each unit should be loaded for minimum total-cost input as the required total output, or system load, varies from the sum of the unit minimum loads of 405 MW to the maximum of 1450 MW.

The procedure is to begin with the lowest incremental rate, then increase it as required to obtain the required total load. Referring to Table 8.4 as well as to Fig. 8.3, the minimum load of 405 MW is obtained at $\lambda = 6.7$. This is the highest lambda at which Unit A can operate at its minimum load, and hence is the system lambda for minimum output of all units. An increase to $\lambda = 7.0$ will obtain the full output of Unit A, giving a system load of 705 MW. The incremental rate must then be increased to 8.15 before Unit B begins to load. From $\lambda = 8.15$ to 8.6, only Unit B's load is increasing. At $\lambda = 8.6$, Unit C begins to load, and at $\lambda = 9.1$ Unit D joins the others. Table 8.4 completes the schedule of unit loadings as system load and lambda increase.

Figure 8.4 is a plot of the loading schedules for each unit as developed in Table 8.4 (with the simplifying assumption of linear loading between breakpoints). Sets of curves such as these, prepared for each possible combination of committed units, could serve as economy loading guides for a generating system. It is apparent, however, that the preparation and use of such curves is

Table 8.4. Loading schedule.

System Load MW	λ $/MWh	Unit Loading, MW				
		A	B	C	D	E
405	6.7	150	120	75	40	20
705	7.0/8.15	450	120	75	40	20
802	8.6	450	217	75	40	20
990	9.1	450	325	155	40	20
1150	9.45	450	400	212	68	20
1310	10.0	450	400	300	112	48
1442	11.0	450	400	300	192	100
1450	11.1	450	400	300	200	100

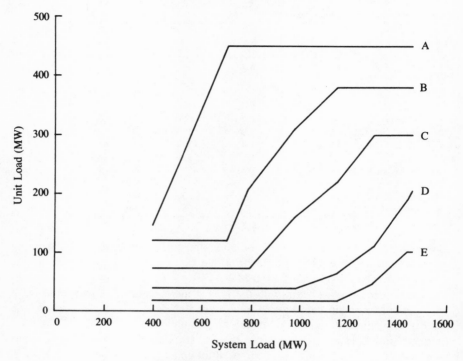

Fig. 8.4. Unit-loading curves.

cumbersome for systems comprising very many generating units, particularly if unit fuel prices change frequently. Hence the trend toward computerized calculation and control of unit loading. Kirchmayer (1958) and others have developed precise algorithms for economic dispatch, not only including the effect of the cost characteristics of generating units, but also allowing for the impact of transmission losses of lines connecting widely separated units.

Hydro Unit Dispatch. The methods used for dispatch of hydro generation vary tremendously, and depend on many factors which are unique to a particular situation. If a utility load is served solely by hydro, dispatch is unrelated to cost, the primary considerations being the assurance of adequate total energy supply, with generating capacity and storage available to meet load demands when they occur. The hydraulic characteristics of the streams and associated dams must be carefully calculated so as to provide energy and capacity even in years of minimum water flow. Added to this complexity may be constraints of minimum and maximum allowable stream flows imposed by navigation, irrigation, flood control, and fishing requirements. It is almost axiomatic that a hydro complex serving as the sole source of power for an electric load cannot be fully developed in the sense of full utilization of head and flow.

As the load of such a system grows beyond the capabilities of the hydro generation, it becomes necessary to add thermal generation to provide energy and capacity in seasons or years when the hydro is deficient. Further load growth requires additional thermal generation, but also permits fuller utilization of the hydro, because now, whenever water is available, the thermal units can be shut down, thus saving fuel and avoiding spilling water over the dams. Ultimately, when the hydro becomes only a small part of the total generation required for the load, it could be allowed to run full-out, generating whatever energy the flow permitted. At this point, however, consideration might be given to altering the characteristics of the hydro to provide more storage and more generating capacity at each site so as to permit greater output at times of system peak load, when thermal units of the highest incremental rate would otherwise be supplying energy.

From the above discussions, it can be seen that hydro dispatch is a complex of considerations involving load, hydraulics, and institutional requirements as well as incremental rates of associated thermal generation. The problems of dispatching hydro-thermal generating systems are discussed in a paper by Drake, Mayall, Kirchmayer, and Wood (1962).

Dispatch of Energy Storage. 'Energy storage,' as used here, refers to storage at the generation level: storage which is operated as, and considered part of, the generating system, and distinct from utilization storage, such as heat storage devices used in connection with space heating of buildings.

The only kind of energy storage in widespread use in generating systems is pumped hydro. A motor-driven pump uses off-peak daily or weekend energy supplied by thermal units at low incremental rates to pump water from a reservoir at one elevation to another at higher elevation. The water is stored until a time of peak load when incremental rates of thermal units are high. The water flows back to the lower reservoir through a hydraulic turbine-generator, thus supplanting high-cost generation.

The round-trip efficiency of a pumped-hydro unit is about 70%, which means that operation is economical if the ratio of incremental costs during the pumping cycle to those at time of generation is less than 0.7. This ratio will vary from day to day, depending on load levels and the costs of thermal units available for commitment. Consequently, it is necessary to plan the operation of storage units several days in advance, anticipating the trend of incremental costs. For details of these procedures, see Marsh, Moisan, and Murrell (1974).

9
System Reliability: Reserves

The needs of operating reliability, discussed in Chapter 8, might suggest the requirement of sufficient installed reserve to permit maintaining the specified operating reserve at all times. Ultimately, however, the objective is not to serve the load with some margin of reserve, but to avoid a condition of negative reserve, which would preclude serving all of the load. Consideration of operating reserve, therefore, is not usually included in the determination of required installed reserve: it is accepted that under extreme conditions of capacity shortage, the system may be without operating reserve for short periods. Actually, the modern approach to reserve, or capacity, planning also accepts the possibility of negative reserve margins, but only on the basis of a calculated probability, given the uncertainties of future load levels and generation availability.

The definition of required reserve margin for a specified system of generation and load characteristics is that which, considering planned and unplanned (forced) outages of generating units and the uncertainties of forecasting future loads, will permit operation of the system with an acceptable risk, or probability, of the existence of an operating condition wherein the load exceeds the generation.

Although electric utility engineers had developed probabilistic methods of reserve determination as early as the 1930s, the huge calculational requirements precluded significant use until the advent of high-speed digital computers in the 1950s. By that time, several alternate methodologies had been developed and were in use in various electric utility systems. One of the earliest, the Loss-of-Load Probability (LOLP) method (Calabrese, 1947; AIEE, 1961), will be discussed in detail. A bibliography by Billinton (1971) gives references to the other methods.

LOSS-OF-LOAD PROBABILITY

The expression 'loss of load' is unfortunate because it suggests a result, whereas all that is meant is a condition of available generation that is less than the forecast load. In operating terms, such a condition may not, in fact, result in cutting off load; and usually does not. Emergency actions, such as voltage or frequency reduction, or purchase from neighboring utilities, may be taken to avoid loss of load in all but the most severe contingencies. This fact, however, does not affect the method's technical usefulness: it is still a rational measure of generating system reliability. The use of the word 'probability' in the name of the method is also unfortunate because it is incorrect: the quantity calculated in this method is, mathematically, an *expected value,* not a probability.

Beyond these quibblings about nomenclature, however, is the fact that LOLP is an acronym familiar to electric utility system engineers in many parts of the world; and the method, or variations of it, is probably more widely used than any other (Allan and Takieddien, 1977).

Forced Outage Probability

The LOLP method uses the outage existence probability of each generating unit, called the 'forced outage rate' (R_f), to calculate the probability of varying amounts of unplanned outage, or nonavailability, of a group of units making up the generating system. In experiential terms, the forced-outage rate of a specific unit is the probability that, on a randomly chosen occasion, one would find the unit unable to operate because it had suffered a failure of some kind which had not yet been repaired. Such outages, as among a group of units, are considered independent events.

It is important to distinguish between the concept of R_f as an *outage existence probability,* suitable for use in an LOLP calculation, and the *statistical* R_f, which is calculated from historical data of existing units or classes of units. Unfortunately, the term 'forced-outage rate' is used for both. Correctly, the generation engineer preparing to make an LOLP calculation should consider statistical R_f data as a basis for estimating the best outage-probability R_f to use in his calculation, depending on the applicability of the data to his own types and sizes of units. One of the most frustrating aspects of generation system reliability analysis is that the newest and largest generating units, whose impacts on reserve requirements are the greatest, inherently have produced the least amount of statistical data from which to form an estimate of forced-outage probability. Here one must rely heavily on experienced judgment.

For purposes of statistical analysis, the Edison Electric Institute of the United States has defined R_f as follows:

$$R_f = \frac{\text{FOH}}{\text{FOH} + \text{SH}}, \tag{9.1}$$

where FOH = Forced-outage hours
        SH = Service hours.

The forced-outage rate as calculated by this equation is considered a good estimator of forced-outage probability for units of the specified size and type *when the data are derived from units operated at high-capacity factor,* i.e. when the sum of FOH and SH is a major fraction of the hours in the period considered. It is a poor estimator when service hours are few, as in peaking units, which typically operate only a few hours per day. An alternate equation (Albrecht, Marsh, and Kindl, 1970) which is applicable to data from units in any kind of service is:

$$R_f = \frac{\text{FOH}(N_h/24)}{\text{FOH}(N_h/24) + \text{SH}}, \tag{9.2}$$

where N_h = Number of service hours per day.

A more rigorous expression is developed in an IEEE Task Group report (1971).

Outage Probability Table

The outage probabilities of all generating units are convolved to produce an outage probability table for the entire system. Table 9.1 gives the derivation of such a table for a three-unit system. The condition of zero outage, for example, requires that all units be in service; so the probability is simply the product of the complements of the forced-outage rates of the three units. For 100 MW of outage, the 100-MW unit must be out, while the other two are in; and so on for all possible combinations of units in and out of service. The fact that the sum of all the probabilities is exactly unity is a check that the mathematics has been performed correctly and that no possible combinations have been omitted.

Table 9.1. Generation outage table.

System Generating Units

Rating, MW	R_f, p.u.	$1 - R_f$
100	0.02	0.98
150	0.03	0.97
200	0.04	0.96

Exact Outage Probabilities

MW of Outage	Probability of Outage
0	$0.98 \times 0.97 \times 0.96 = 0.912576$
100	$0.02 \times 0.97 \times 0.96 = 0.018624$
150	$0.98 \times 0.03 \times 0.96 = 0.028224$
200	$0.98 \times 0.97 \times 0.04 = 0.038024$
250	$0.02 \times 0.03 \times 0.96 = 0.000576$
300	$0.02 \times 0.97 \times 0.04 = 0.000776$
350	$0.98 \times 0.03 \times 0.04 = 0.001176$
450	$0.02 \times 0.03 \times 0.04 = 0.000024$
	1.000000

Table 9.2. Cumulative generation outage table.

MW or More of Outage	Probability
0	1.000000
100	0.087424
150	0.068800
200	0.040576
250	0.002552
300	0.001976
350	0.001200
450	0.000024

The complete outage table for a system of twenty or thirty units contains millions of entries, which explains why digital computers are a necessity for any practical use of the method. Even so, it has been necessary to develop special computational techniques to build the table in probability sequence from highest to lowest, truncating the table at probability values such as 10^{-15}. Table 9.2 contains the same data as Table 9.1, but in cumulative form, which is more convenient for the LOLP calculation.

LOLP Calculation

In making an LOLP calculation for a one-year period, the first step is to recognize that, because of scheduled maintenance, not all installed units will be available continuously throughout the year. Maintenance periods are established, usually integral numbers of weeks, and each unit's required maintenance outage is assigned to a specific period of the year so as to fill the seasonal load-drop area as described in Chapter 8 and Fig. 8.1. The result of this process is the identification of specific groups of units, each of which will be considered available (not scheduled out of service) to serve the loads of one of the maintenance periods. For each of these groups, a cumulative outage table is calculated, similar to Table 9.2. The outage tables for a year are referred to as the 'capacity model.'

The next step is to calculate the available reserve for each day of each maintenance period. This is simply the difference between the available capacity in the maintenance period and the peak hourly load of each day. The probability of insufficient capacity (loss-of-load probability) for each day is then obtained from the cumulative outage table as that one probability whose associated 'outage-or-more' is just greater than the available reserve. The LOLP for the period is then:

$$\text{LOLP} = \sum_1^n p_\text{d},$$ (9.3)

where p_d = loss-of-load probability for each day
n = number of days in the period.

LOLP for the year is obtained by summing the values for each period. The sequence or list of daily peak loads covering a year's time is usually called a 'load model.' When probability calculations are made for a series of years, frequently the best estimate is that the daily peak loads of all the years will be proportionate to the growth of load, in which case the load model is prepared in per unit of the annual peak load. This permits characterizing a system's LOLP in terms of its installed capacity and annual peak load only.

A typical value of LOLP for purposes of reserve determination of a large interconnection is 0.1, which, as an expected value, has units of days per year. It is not unusual to quote LOLP in inverse units, i.e. '10 years per day' or 'one day in 10 years.'

The uncertainty of future forecast loads may be accounted for if a probability distribution of loads can be defined. The procedure then is to repeat the LOLP calculation for several load points on the distribution curve and obtain a prob-ability-weighted sum as the LOLP for the year. Because of the exponential character of the outage table, the inclusion of load uncertainty usually increases the LOLP, and hence, the reserve margin required for a stipulated value of LOLP.

Examples of the use of the LOLP calculation in a total system economic study are given in Chapter 11.

INTERPRETATION OF LOLP

LOLP, as calculated by eqn (9.3), is described as an expected value. The rationale for this is that if p_d for some one day were 100%, one would *expect* one day of failure to serve the load; and this idea is extended to saying that if $p_d < 100\%$, one would expect a fractional part of a day of failure; and that if there were many such fractional parts of a day of failure during the course of a year, the sum of the fractional days is the number of days of failure one would expect for the year. Equation (9.3), then, is not summing probabilities, but *probable days* of failure.

The mathematical concept of expected value is not as familiar to most people as that of probability, or chance. For example, if one were to be told by the owner of a racehorse that he expected Bright Light to place somewhere between first and second, perhaps 1.6, in next Saturday's race, it would be interesting information, but not very useful. If, on the other hand, Bright Light's owner were to say, 'There's a 90 percent chance that he'll win,' one would have the basis, at least, for a nine-to-one wager.

Yearly Probability

The chances of success of a generating system can also be calculated, using the daily loss-of-load probabilities which are the basis of LOLP. If we define a yearly reliability, R_y, as the probability of getting through a year without a day of insufficient capacity,

$$R_y = \prod_{d=1}^{n} (1 - p_d),$$ (9.4)

which is the product of the complements of the daily loss-of-load probabilities, and amounts to the probability of success. If the p_d's were all equal,

$$R_y = (1 - p_d)^n.$$ (9.5)

In generation systems, daily probabilities are never all equal, and the practical difficulty of performing the multiplications of eqn (9.4) in the time of the early reliability investigators may well have had some influence on their decision to calculate expected value rather than probability of success or failure. Even with today's computers, eqn (9.4) is time-consuming and expensive, and accordingly is not used. However, eqn (9.5) provides a means for a close approximation of the value of R_y within the range of variation of p_d encountered in practical cases, and for values of R_y that are of interest.

The approximation consists of obtaining an average value of p_d by dividing LOLP by the number of days per year:

$$p_d = \frac{\text{LOLP}}{n}.$$ (9.6)

Substituting eqn (9.6) in eqn (9.5) gives:

$$R_y = \left(1 - \frac{\text{LOLP}}{n}\right)^n.$$ (9.7)

In this context, n is the number of *effective* days per year, i.e. the number of days whose real p_d contributes significantly to the total LOLP. It is not really necessary in most cases to have any knowledge of the number of effective days, because they are ordinarily in the range of 25 to 365 days, and for LOLP as high as 2, there is very little difference whether R_y is calculated using $n = 25$ or $n = 365$.

For a typical LOLP value of 0.1, eqn (9.7) gives $R_y = 0.9047$ if $n = 25$; $R_y = 0.9048$ if $n = 365$. In either case, the chance of getting through the year without a day of insufficient capacity is about 90%.

EFFECTIVE LOAD–CARRYING CAPACITY

The effective load-carrying capacity (or, simply, effective capacity) of a generating *system* is defined as the annual peak load (assuming a given per unit load model) that the system can serve at a specified value of LOLP (or any other index of reliability). In Fig. 9.1, the effective capacity of the original system at LOLP $= 0.1$ is given at Point A. With a unit added, it is at Point B. The

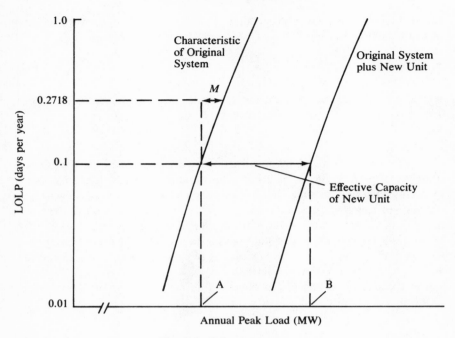

Fig. 9.1. Effective capacity.

effective capacity of a generating *unit* is the difference between the effective capacity of the system with and without the unit installed, or included in the outage probability table. In Fig. 9.1, the effective capacity of the new unit is the horizontal distance between the two characteristic curves, measured at LOLP = 0.1. Although the *system* effective capacity is critical as to the risk index chosen, the near-parallel shape of the curves causes the *unit* effective capacity to be relatively insensitive to the chosen LOLP within one or two orders of magnitude.

The effective capacity of a unit may be found graphically as in Fig. 9.1, but for many purposes, the approximation of Garver (1966) is entirely adequate:

$$L = C - M \ln(1 - R_f + R_f e^{C/M}), \qquad (9.8)$$

where L = unit effective capacity, MW
$\quad C$ = unit rated capacity, MW
$\quad M$ = slope characteristic, MW
$\quad \ln$ = natural logarithm
$\quad R_f$ = unit forced-outage rate, p.u.
$\quad e$ = Naperian constant, 2.718. . . .

The slope characteristic, M, is best obtained from the system characteristic curve of LOLP versus annual peak load. It is the change in system effective capacity when the LOLP changes by the factor, e, as shown in Fig. 9.1. It is measured at the chosen value of LOLP. If necessary, M may be roughly estimated to be in the range of 3% to 5% of system capacity for isolated systems of 10 000 MW to 1000 MW. If a small system is interconnected with others in an agreement for pooling reserves and mutual support in emergency outages, the value of M should be based on the total capacity of the interconnected systems.

Also, if M is known for a system at some value of LOLP, a fair estimate of M at increased capacity and the same LOLP is given by:

$$M_2 = M_1 \times \text{Cap}_2 \times \text{Res}_2/(\text{Cap}_1 \times \text{Res}_1), \qquad (9.9)$$

where M_1, M_2 = base and new M, MW

$\text{Cap}_1, \text{Cap}_2$ = base and new system capacity, MW

$\text{Res}_1, \text{Res}_2$ = base and new reserve, percent of system
effective capacity at constant LOLP.

SUMMARY

LOLP is a probabilistic method of measuring the reliability of a utility generating system with respect to a load to be served. It is widely used as a rational method for establishing required reserve level. The steps of a LOLP calculation are as follows:

1. Estimate, from historical data, the forced-outage rates to be expected for each unit of the system. One source of American historical data is the Edison Electric Institute (EEI, 1977).*
2. Divide the year into a convenient number of maintenance periods and assign each unit to one or more contiguous periods so as to approximate its required maintenance time. Schedule the largest amount of capacity on maintenance to the times of year when peak loads are lowest. See Fig. 8.1.
3. Using the methods of Tables 9.1 and 9.2, calculate outage probability tables for each maintenance period in the year.
4. List the peak loads for each day in each maintenance period.
5. Subtract each load from the capacity available (i.e. not scheduled for maintenance) in its maintenance period, giving the available reserve. For each available reserve enter the cumulative outage table at the first outage larger than the reserve; record the associated probability. Sum the probabilities for the year, giving annual LOLP in days per year.

The concept of effective capacity is useful in approximate comparisons of the system reliability and the forced-outage-rate effects of alternate unit additions to a generating system. It may also be used to approximate LOLP calculations of an expanding system, as described in Garver (1966).

* In the future, data will be prepared and published by the National Electric Reliability Council.

10

Economic Characteristics
of Generating Units

The economic characteristics of a generating unit are those which determine the cost at which it produces electrical energy. This cost will be discussed in terms of three components: cost of fuel, cost of operation and maintenance, and capital, or investment, cost. The first two of these are frequently combined and referred to as 'production costs.'

FUEL COST OF GENERATION

The fuel cost of generation with respect to a particular unit is measured in mills per kWh (or dollars per MWh, which has the same numeric value). It is the product of a unit heat rate expressed in kJ/kWh (Btu/kWh) and a fuel price expressed in $/GJ ($/MBtu),* with appropriate scale factors applied. The first question to be considered pertains to the heat rate, or efficiency, of generating units.

Efficiency is the dimensionless ratio of output to input. Heat rate is the inverse ratio, but with input expressed in heat units and output in electric energy units. Thus, in the SI system, heat rate and efficiency are related by:

$$\text{Heat Rate } (h) = \frac{3600}{\eta}, \text{ in kJ/kWh.} \tag{10.1}$$

---

*MBtu is a commonly used mixture of Système International (SI) and U.S. units where M is the prefix *mega*, meaning the factor 10^6. This should not be confused with the Roman numeral M (1000), commonly used in fuel gas measurements, e.g. *Mcf* (1000 cubic feet). Occasionally encountered is the unit MMBtu, which is intended to mean 10^6 Btu, but which is meaningless in the SI system and stands for 2000 Btu in the Roman system.

In U.S. units,

$$h = \frac{3412.14}{\eta} \text{ , in Btu/kWh,} \tag{10.2}$$

where η = efficiency in per unit.

Regardless of whether one is considering a generating unit's performance in terms of efficiency or of heat rate, it is important to specify the conditions of both input and output. These conditions are determined by many factors, but it will be convenient to categorize them according to the type of fuel burned: fossil or nuclear.

Fossil-Fuel Cycles

Coal and oil and natural gas are usually measured by unit of mass or volume; but for costing purposes it is necessary to know the cost by unit of heating value, and this requires a digression into the subject of the heating values of fossil fuels.

Fossil-Fuel Heating Value. The heat of combustion of fossil fuels is derived from the oxidation of carbon, hydrogen, and, to a lesser extent, sulfur. If the heating value is measured with a bomb calorimeter, the products of combustion of the sample are reduced to room temperature, with the result that the water formed from combustion of hydrogen is in liquid form. However, in any practical combustion device, such as a boiler or the combustion system of a gas turbine, it is not possible to reduce the products of combustion to a temperature low enough to condense the water vapor produced from combustion of hydrogen. Hence, for practical purposes, the heat of vaporization of product water is unavailable to any thermodynamic process: it is lost up the stack with the water vapor.

This fact has given rise to the practice of defining two heating values for fossil fuels: a 'higher (gross) heating value' (HHV), as measured by the bomb calorimeter, and a 'lower (net) heating value' (LHV), in which the heat of vaporization of water has been subtracted. The distinction is important in considering the efficiency of combustion devices because the calculated efficiency will be higher or lower, according to whether the lower or higher heating value is used as input.

Fossil fuels vary in their relative proportions of hydrogen, hence the ratios HHV/LHV also vary. The usual ranges are:

Coal	1.03–1.04
Oil	1.06–1.07
Natural Gas	1.10–1.11

Designers and manufacturers of combustion equipment tend to prefer to use LHV because calculated efficiencies are (in this respect) independent of the type of fuel to be used. Users of such equipment, however, may find it more convenient to use HHV because that is the more frequently used base for fuel-purchase specifications. So long as efficiency and fuel price per unit of heating value are expressed on the same base, the calculated fuel cost per kWh is independent of base. In making comparisons of unit efficiency or heat rate, or of fuel prices, it is necessary to ascertain whether a common heating value base is used.

In the United States and Great Britain, utilities use the higher heating value. Elsewhere, practice is divided. In this book higher heating values are used unless otherwise stated.

The ranges of higher heating values of fossil fuels are, approximately,

Coal	18–33 GJ/t (7700–14 000 Btu/lb)
Oil	42–47 GJ/t (18 000–20 000 Btu/lb)
Natural Gas	34–41 MJ/m³(900–1100 Btu/ft³)

Fossil-Steam Unit Heat Rates. The diagram of Fig. 10.1 illustrates the principal losses of a fossil-fired steam unit, and realistic values, assuming heat input from combustion of fuel to be 100 arbitrary power units. Chimney, or stack, loss occurs because it is not practical to cool the products of combustion below about 120°C (250°F). The boiler efficiency is 87% in this example.

The turbine-generator input is 87, and this, less the windage, friction, electrical, and condenser losses, leaves a gross output at the generator terminals of 38. The turbine gross efficiency is 38/87 = 43.68%. This corresponds to a 'turbine gross heat rate' of 8242 kJ/kWh (7812 Btu/kWh). In Fig. 10.1, the boiler feed pump is assumed to be electrically driven, and when this power is subtracted, the 'turbine net heat rate' is obtained—in this case, 8700 kJ/kWh (8246 Btu/kWh). In many cases, particularly in larger units, the boiler feed pump is driven by a small steam turbine incorporated into the steam cycle of the main turbine; in such cases the turbine gross and net heat rates are indistinguishable.

The 'net unit heat rate' (usually referred to as 'net station heat rate') includes the effect of boiler losses and auxiliary power. The latter is the power required to drive all unit fans and pumps (other than the boiler feed pump) and the pro-rata share (in a multi-unit station) of general station service power. In Fig. 10.1, the net unit efficiency is 35% and the net unit heat rate, 10 286 kJ/kWh (9749 Btu/kWh).

While this heat rate terminology is not universal, the physical facts of Fig. 10.1 are. Hence it is important to clearly define terms when quoting heat rates so as to avoid, for example, confusing a turbine heat rate and a net station heat rate, since these can differ by 25% or more.

In the context of the heat rates discussed in Chapter 8 (Fig. 8.2), the heat rates discussed here are total heat rates at the full-load point. In economic analyses, only net unit heat rates are of interest, because it is the aggregate of net unit output which is construed to be the 'load' served by a system of

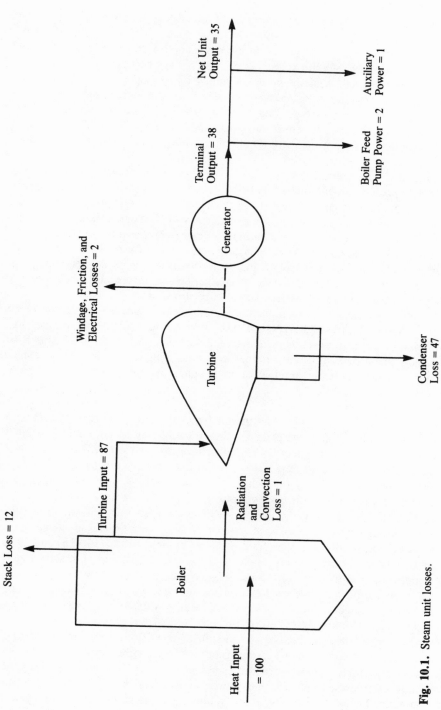

Fig. 10.1. Steam unit losses.

generating units. In absolute terms, net unit full-load heat rates of fossil units vary from a low of about 9000 kJ/kWh (8530 Btu/kWh) to 19 000 kJ/kWh (18 000 Btu/kWh). The high end of the range applies only to existing, very old units. New units seldom exceed 12 500 kJ/kWh (11 850 Btu/kWh). Part-load, hence incremental, heat rates vary significantly among generating units, depending on the characteristics of the steam cycle, the boiler, the turbine, and the auxiliary power system. Heat rates at any load depend upon the turbine exhaust pressure (or condenser vacuum), which varies with the temperature of the condenser cooling medium, which in turn may change with the seasons.

Internal-Combustion Unit Heat Rates. The basic input-output principles of Fig. 10.1 apply also to internal-combustion prime movers, which in utility applications are represented primarily by gas turbines and diesel engines. These prime movers, however, are integrated in such a way that the efficiencies of the combustion, heat-transfer, and turbine (engine) components cannot easily be individually recognized; hence only an overall unit efficiency may be quoted, from fuel input to electrical output. The consideration of higher and lower heating values of fuel is pertinent; and auxiliary power losses must be considered, although their magnitude is less than that of steam units.

Net station heat rates of modern simple-cycle gas turbines are in the range of 10 600 to 12 100 kJ/kWh (10 050 to 11 470 Btu/kWh). More complex gas turbine cycles and diesel engines may approach 9700 kJ/kWh (9200 Btu/kWh) full-load heat rate. Both gas turbines and diesel engines suffer reduced output capability with increased ambient air temperature, and this is reflected in slightly increased heat rate.

Combined-Cycle Efficiency. Any thermodynamic process consists of heating a working fluid to a high temperature, then cooling it in a heat engine (turbine) to produce mechanical energy. The higher the 'top' temperature, and the lower the 'bottom' temperature, the more efficient the conversion process. (The maximum possible efficiency of a thermodynamic cycle is that of the ideal, or Carnot, cycle, whose efficiency equals $(T_1 - T_2)/T_1$, where T_1 and T_2 are the absolute temperatures of the inlet and exhaust, respectively.) In the pursuit of higher efficiency, engineers have found that the economic and practical limits for the most common working fluid, steam, are about 540°C (1000°F) and 27°C (80°F). Other working fluids, such as air, permit the design of practical heat engines using top temperatures much higher than those of steam cycles, but do not allow recovery, or conversion to mechanical energy, of the lower end of the temperature range. A simple-cycle gas turbine, for example, may operate between 1100°C (2010°F) and 540°C (1000°F).

The temperature at which heat is lost, or rejected from a gas turbine, is thus at a level suitable for input to a steam turbine. By combining the two working fluids in a single cycle, the entire temperature range of both fluids may be utilized with consequent efficiency improvement. The resulting cycle is called a 'combined cycle.' It consists of the 'topping cycle' and the 'bottoming cycle.'

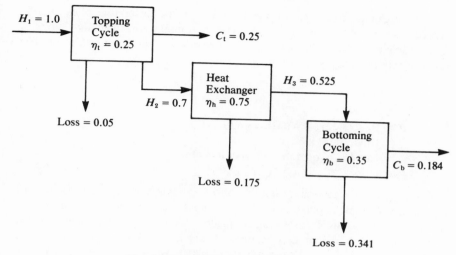

Fig. 10.2. Combined-cycle efficiency.

Figure 10.2 is an idealized representation of a combined cycle showing how an improvement in overall efficiency may be obtained by combining two cycles of moderate efficiency. The heat, H_1, is converted by the topping cycle of efficiency $\eta_t = 0.25$ to output $C_t = 0.25$. The heat rejection of the topping cycle, H_2, becomes input to a heat exchanger, which transfers heat from one working fluid to another at efficiency $\eta_h = 0.75$. The heat exchanger output, H_3, becomes the input to the bottoming cycle, which, with an efficiency of $\eta_b = 0.35$, produces output $C_b = 0.184$. The resulting combined-cycle efficiency is given by:

$$\eta_{cc} = (C_t + C_b)/H_1 = (0.25 + 0.184)/1.0 = 0.434. \qquad (10.3)$$

A commercially-available expression of the combined cycle is the combined gas turbine–steam turbine cycle, which, burning natural gas or oil, can produce an efficiency of about 42%, corresponding to a net station heat rate of 8571 kJ/kWh (8124 Btu/kWh). This is the highest efficiency available for generating units burning these fuels. Under development is a cycle with integrated low-Btu gasifier which may permit direct use of coal fuel with an efficiency higher than that of conventional coal-fired steam units having comparable air- and water-pollution control capability.

In the past, successful combined cycles were built using mercury-vapor turbines topping steam turbines, although none now remain in service. Magnetohydrodynamic (MHD) generators or potassium-vapor turbines topping conventional steam turbines represent potential future developments for higher efficiency in the conversion of heat into electrical energy.

Fossil-Fuel Inventory Cost. Sometimes neglected, but nevertheless a part of the total fuel cost of a generating unit, is the carrying charge, or financing cost of the investment in inventory, or stock, of fuel at the generating plant site. In order to assure continuous supply, it is common practice to maintain a stock of fuel sufficient for 60 to 90 days full-load operation of the units in a plant. The value of this inventory is given by:

$$V_f = h \times C \times 24 \times N_f \times F/10^6, \tag{10.4}$$

where V_f = Value of inventory, \$
$\qquad h$ = Heat rate, kJ/kWh (Btu/kWh)
$\qquad C$ = Unit rating, kW
$\qquad N_f$ = Number of operating days of inventory
$\qquad F$ = Price of fuel, \$/GJ (\$/MBtu).

For so long as a generating unit is considered available and operable as part of a utility system, it must have an inventory of fuel, whether it runs or not. The inventory is thus a current asset, made necessary by the existence of the generating unit. Its value may change as fuel of one price is consumed and replaced with fuel of a different price; but it is never used up, and it does not depreciate in value solely with time or use. It is, like land, a nondepreciable asset whose financing cost is a part of total generating cost.

The annual cost of fuel inventory is its average value multiplied by the fixed-charge rate for nondepreciable assets. Although a fixed cost in the sense that it is not directly dependent on the operation of the generating unit, it is usually categorized and shown as part of fuel cost. It may be expressed in \$ per year, or normalized to the rating of the unit and expressed as \$/kW-yr.

Example of Fossil Unit Fuel Cost. The following example illustrates the calculation of fossil unit fuel cost.

Assumed Data:
Unit Rating:	100 MW
Full-Load Heat Rate:	10 500 kJ/kWh
	(9953 Btu/kWh)
Fuel Price:	1.5 \$/GJ (1.58 \$/MBtu)
Operation:	6000 hr per year at full load
Inventory:	60 days
Nondepreciable Fixed-Charge Rate:	0.12

\$/MWh Fuel Cost:
$\qquad (10\ 500\ \text{kJ/kWh}) \times (1.5 \times 10^{-6}\text{\$/kJ}) \times 1000 = 15.75\ \text{\$/MWh}$

Annual Fuel Cost:
$\qquad (15.75\ \text{\$/MWh}) \times (100\ \text{MW}) \times (6000\ \text{hr/yr}) \times 10^{-6} = 9.45\ \text{M\$/yr}$

Inventory Cost:
From eqn (10.4):

$$V_f = 10\ 500 \times 100\ 000 \times 24 \times 60 \times 1.5 \times 10^{-6} \times 10^{-6}$$
$$= 2.268\ \text{M\$}$$

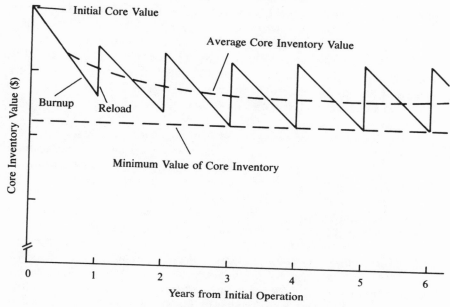

Fig. 10.3. Nuclear reactor core value.

Annual Inventory Cost $= 0.12 \times 2.268 = 0.27$ M\$/yr

Total Annual Fuel Cost $= 9.45 + 0.27 = 9.72$ M\$/yr.

Note that the annual inventory cost is less than 3% of the total annual fuel cost in this example.

Nuclear Fuel-Cycle Cost

The cost of fuel of a nuclear unit is calculated in the same way as that of a fossil unit: a cost per kWh representing the fuel actually consumed, and an annual carrying charge, or required return on the inventory investment. The relative magnitudes of the two components are quite different, however; and there is a much greater degree of approximation in the reduction of the complex nuclear fuel-cycle cash flows to an effective cost per unit of heating value as burned.

Nuclear Fuel Inventory. One of the major characteristics of the nuclear fuel cycle is its very large fuel inventory. A certain minimum quantity of fuel must reside in the core of the reactor to maintain the level of reactivity and heat release required for rated output. This is quite different from the fossil-fired unit, where the fuel inventory is related only to convenience and assurance of uninterrupted supply. Further, the size of the required nuclear fuel inventory corresponds to twelve to eighteen months of full-load operation, as contrasted to two to three months for fossil units.

Figure 10.3 is an idealized plot of core fuel value typical of a light-water-moderated-and-cooled reactor (LWR) operating on a yearly refueling cycle with slightly enriched uranium fuel. The initial core consists entirely of 'new' fuel. During the first year of operation, as heat is produced through nuclear fission, steam is generated to operate a conventional steam turbine and generator. The reactivity, hence the heating value and the dollar value, is correspondingly reduced. At the end of the first year, a portion—between 25% and 33%—of the core is removed and replaced with fresh fuel, allowing the reactor to operate for another year.

This process is repeated each year until, by the fourth or fifth year, the core has reached 'equilibrium,' a condition wherein it has a more or less uniform distribution of new and partially-spent fuel. This procedure results in higher fuel costs in the early years of the reactor's life, but reduces the average value of core inventory in later years. Once the core has reached equilibrium, it operates between the minimum value necessary for rated output and the value necessary to provide enough fuel for a full year's operation.

Nuclear reactors of different types and designs vary in their requirements for minimum core inventory and in the kind and frequency of their reload cycles. Figure 10.3 merely illustrates the principle by which an equivalent average inventory may be obtained for use in fuel-cost calculations. As with fossil fuel, the annual inventory cost is the product of the average value of the inventory and the fixed-charge rate for nondepreciable assets.

Nuclear Fuel Burnup Cost. The reduction in fuel inventory value each year, as shown in Fig. 10.3, is a measure of the cost of heat input to the nuclear steam cycle. It is commonly called the 'burnup' cost. If the reactor of Fig. 10.3 is assumed to operate at full-load continuously, then the horizontal scale is also a measure of heat generated. The slope of the line captioned 'burnup' thus has the dimensions $/GJ ($/MBtu). This then represents an equivalent 'price' of nuclear fuel, and it may be used in generating cost calculations precisely as the price of fossil fuel is used. The changing slope as the reactor approaches the equilibrium state is handled by converting to a level equivalent uniform series using present-worth methods.

Example of Nuclear Fuel Cost. The following example of nuclear fuel-cycle cost calculation is based on cost levels estimated to be appropriate to the mid-1980s time period.

Assumed Data:

Unit Rating:	1000 MW
Burnup Cost:	0.80 $/GJ (0.844 $/MBtu)
Inventory Value:	80 $/kW
Nondepreciable Fixed-Charge Rate:	0.12
Heat Rate:	10 970 kJ/kWh (10 398 Btu/kWh)
Operation:	6000 hr per year at full load

$/MWh Burnup Cost:

$$(10\ 970\ \text{kJ/kWh}) \times (0.80 \times 10^{-6}\ \$/\text{kJ}) \times 1000 = 8.78\ \$/\text{MWh}$$

Annual Burnup Cost:

$$(8.78 \times 10^{-3}\ \$/\text{kWh}) \times (10^6\ \text{kW}) \times (6000\ \text{hr/yr}) \times 10^{-6} = 52.66\ \text{M\$/yr}$$

Annual Inventory Cost:

$$(80\$/\text{kW}) \times (10^6\ \text{kW}) \times (0.12) \times 10^{-6} = 9.6\ \text{M\$/yr}$$

$$\text{Total Annual Fuel Cost} = 52.66 + 9.6 = 62.26\ \text{M\$/yr}.$$

Note that the nuclear fuel inventory cost is about 15% of total fuel cost in this typical example.

In some economic studies, it is convenient, and sufficiently accurate, to combine the burnup and inventory costs into a single cost, usually expressed in $/GJ ($/MBtu). In the above example, the inventory cost per kWh is:

$$(9.6 \times 10^6\ \$/\text{yr})/(6000\ \text{hr} \times 10^6\ \text{kW}) = 0.0016\ \$/\text{kWh}.$$

If this cost had been incurred by fuel burnup at the unit heat rate, the equivalent burnup cost would be:

$$(0.0016\ \$/\text{kWh})/10\ 970\ \text{kJ/kWh} = 0.146 \times 10^{-6}\ \$/\text{kJ, or } 0.146\ \$/\text{GJ}.$$

This may be added to the real burnup cost of 0.80 $/GJ to give the total fuel-cycle cost of 0.945 $/GJ (0.997 $/MBtu).

This total cost may be used with the unit heat rate to give correct fuel-cycle cost in $/MWh or $/yr if the operating hours are exactly 6000 per year and the unit operates only at its full-load heat rate. For other operating hours and loadings, the inventory component will be in error; but since it amounts only to about 15% of the total, the approximation is, for some purposes, acceptable.

OPERATION AND MAINTENANCE COST

Operation and maintenance (O&M) costs logically divide into two categories: (1) those which are 'fixed,' in the sense of being relatively independent of the extent of operation of the generating unit, and (2) those which are approximately direct functions of the energy output of the unit, called 'variable.' The former are measured in dollars per year, or, when normalized to the unit rating, in $/kW-yr. The latter are expressed in $/MWh of energy generated.

In the fixed category falls the labor cost of operators and maintenance personnel necessary to the normal operation of the unit and in regular attendance at the generating station. Also included are a pro-rata share of the station's administrative personnel and miscellaneous supply costs.

The variable category includes the cost of replacement parts, lubricants, and other supplies whose consumption is occasioned by the fact that the unit has operated. In addition, some maintenance procedures and inspections may be performed on a schedule related to hours of unit operation; and if nonassigned maintenance crews are brought to the station to perform this work, their cost would be in the variable category.

While it is possible thus to categorize O&M costs, it is not always possible to obtain reliable data for use in economic studies. This is because costs are so much a function of the type of unit, its size or rating, and the disparate O&M practices of utility organizations, particularly with respect to preventive maintenance. Some general observations can be made, however.

Steam Unit O&M Cost

The annual cost for operation and maintenance of a fossil or nuclear unit in base-load service is of the order of 1% to 2% of its capital cost. Most of this cost—perhaps as much as 80%—is in the fixed category, and for this reason it is not uncommon in economic studies to make the simplifying assumption that all of the O&M cost is fixed.

O&M costs (per unit of output) of steam units are inversely proportional to the size of unit. A 100-MW unit does not, for example, require twice as many operators as a 50-MW unit. It is common to express this relationship in an exponential law of the following form:

$$O = O_0(C_0/C)^x, \tag{10.5}$$

where O = O&M cost of new unit, \$/yr/kW
     O_0 = O&M cost of base unit, \$/yr/kW
     C = Rating of new unit, kW
     C_0 = Rating of base unit, kW
     x = Characteristic exponent

This exponential characteristic is sometimes expressed in terms of a 'D-factor' (doubling factor). The D-factor (K_d) is the per unit reduction in cost when unit size doubles. That is, $O = (1 - K_d)O_0$ when $C = 2C_0$. Substituting these values in eqn (10.5),

$$1 - K_d = (0.5)^x$$

and

$$x = \log(1 - K_d)/\log 0.5. \tag{10.6}$$

Substituting in (10.5):

$$O = O_0(C_0/C)^{\log(1 - K_d)/\log 0.5}. \tag{10.7}$$

A typical value of K_d is 0.2, which corresponds to $x = 0.322$.

Internal-Combustion Unit O&M Cost

Internal-combustion units in general, and gas turbines in particular, tend to be designed for unattended operation with remote control, which greatly reduces their fixed components of O&M cost. Furthermore, an inherent characteristic of this kind of machinery is the need for replacement of wearable parts, such as piston rings, valves, and combustion-chamber liners, all as a function of operating hours. Consequently, the largest part of internal-combustion unit O&M cost is variable, expressed usually in $/MWh. Frequently the fixed portion is ignored in economic analyses. As would be expected, there is little variation in cost purely as a function of unit size.

UNIT CAPITAL COST

(The capital-cost component of a generating unit is its value as capitalized and entered into the plant asset account of the company's books at the time it goes into commercial service) It includes all expenditures made prior to and during the construction period for architect and engineer's services, equipment, materials, construction labor, and construction management. As discussed in Chapter 3, it may also include a nominal interest charge on funds used (invested) during the construction period, and called 'interest during construction' (IDC). (Unit capital cost is the number to which it is appropriate to apply the fixed-charge rate to obtain the annual revenue requirement for capital during the productive life of the unit)

Plant Cost Estimates

Although the word 'plant' may connote a generating station consisting of more than one unit, the term 'plant cost' will, in accordance with common parlance, be here construed to mean the capital cost, as defined above, of a single unit of a generating station. It is important to distinguish among units in a station because differences in rating, design, and year of installation make the capital cost of each unit unique and generally not comparable to others in the station.

In generation economic studies, one is usually dealing with units to be installed at some future time, which makes it necessary to estimate future, not current, plant costs. The conventional way of doing this is to start with a detailed cost estimate using known materials and labor costs for the present year. This would be the cost if the plant could be built instantaneously, as it were. A construction schedule is then developed, from which an estimate is made of year-by-year expenditures throughout the construction period.

Inflation and Interest During Construction

Table 10.1 illustrates how a base-year cost estimate may be projected into the plant capital cost as of the first year of service. Construction is assumed to start at the beginning of year 1, and since this is a capital investment, the cost estimates are quoted as of that time. Construction continues through the end of year 7, and the accumulated costs thus become the total plant cost as of the beginning of year 8, which is the first year of operation. The estimated total

Table 10.1. Unit capital cost: 7-year construction period.

Expenditure Year	Base- Cost Estimate	Years of Inflation	Inflated Cost at 6%/year	Years of IDC	IDC Cost at 10%	Total Cost
(1)	(2)	(3)	(4)	(5)	(6)	(7)
1	5	0.5	5.15	6.5	3.35	8.50
2	15	1.5	16.37	5.5	9.00	25.37
3	20	2.5	23.14	4.5	10.41	33.55
4	20	3.5	24.52	3.5	8.58	33.10
5	20	4.5	26.00	2.5	6.50	32.50
6	15	5.5	20.67	1.5	3.10	23.77
7	5	6.5	7.30	0.5	0.37	7.67
Year 8 Totals	100		123.15		41.31	164.46

plant cost as of year 1 is 100, and in the absence of inflation or interest during construction (IDC), this would be the cost as of year 8 also. The expenditure schedule, shown in column 2 of Table 10.1 is 5, 15, 20, 20, 20, 15, and 5 for the seven years of the construction period.

In considering the inflation of these expenditures, it must be recalled that the investment costs are quoted as of the beginning of each year, while the expenditures are actually spread throughout the year. To approximate this situation, the first year's costs are inflated only one half-year, the second year's one and one-half, and so forth, as shown in column 3.

Using a rate of 6% per year, Column 4 gives the actual inflated expenditures. For example, the expenditure in year 3 is: $20 \times (1.06)^{2.5} = 23.14$. The total of column 4 is the actual cost of the plant as of the end of year 7, or the beginning of year 8.

If the practice is to impute an interest cost of funds used during construction and include it in the plant capital cost, columns 5 and 6 of Table 10.1 give the necessary calculations, using an IDC rate of 10% and the same half-year convention as for inflation. Note that in this example the interest during construction is not compounded; e.g., the IDC for the expenditure of year 3 is $4.5 \times 0.1 \times 23.14 = 10.41$. Column 7 gives the totals by which the final plant cost of 164.46 is determined.

This is the plant cost as of (the beginning of) year 8. Note that the cost of 100, estimated at the beginning of year 1, is not a real plant cost. It is not the cost of a plant which would go into service in year 1. Such a plant would have to begin construction seven years earlier, and its construction expenditures would be correspondingly deflated. It is not necessary to redo Table 10.1 to obtain the correct cost of a year-1 plant, however. It is simply the year-8 cost deflated seven years, or $164.46/(1.06)^7 = 109.38$. Once a plant cost, including inflation and interest during construction, has been calculated as of some year, it may be translated to any other year in this way, assuming inflation and IDC rates remain fixed.

The cumulative values of columns 2, 4, and 7 of Table 10.1 are shown

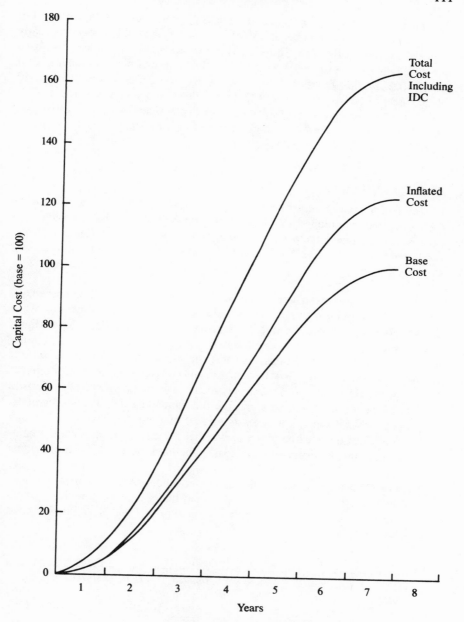

Fig. 10.4. Unit capital cost.

graphically in Fig. 10.4. The large impact on plant capital cost of IDC is clearly evident and suggests the importance of minimizing construction time. However, if the desired year of commercial operation is considered fixed, as it logically is, the impact of inflation is greater for a shorter construction period. For example, if construction is begun in year 4, and a comparable pattern of yearly expenditure distribution (15, 35, 35, 15) used, the base-cost estimate will have inflated by a factor of $(1.06)^3 = 1.191$, with the results given in column 2 of Table 10.2. Further inflation during the construction period makes the inflated plant cost 134.02, contrasted to 123.15 for the seven-year case. The IDC is less—26.14 compared to 41.31—but the total plant cost is only slightly less: 160.16 compared to 164.46. Short construction time may thus be a mixed blessing in an inflationary economy.

Plant Cost Definition

It is quite common to express plant costs in $/kW, and this is a useful device for discussion and comparison of generating units. But, as with any such ratio (kJ/kWh is another example), misleading impressions and conclusions may result if definitions of either numerator or denominator are unstated or imprecisely stated.

Plant Cost Components. There are some components of a generating unit whose costs, logically and obviously, must always be included in the numerator of the $/kW figure: the boiler, the turbine generator, their auxiliaries, the auxiliary power system, the control system, the buildings housing the boiler and turbine-generator, and their foundations, to name the major ones. Moving backwards (in the sense of the energy flow through the unit), there is equipment for moving fuel from on-site storage to the unit, equipment which may serve other units at the site as well. There will be extensive fuel unloading and storage facilities, common to several units, whose costs may or may not be apportioned among units. Consideration must be given to whether the cost of land, station administrative buildings, and general maintenance facilities are included in individual unit costs.

A major element in the variability of unit-cost constituents is environmental-control equipment, such as cooling towers and flue-gas cleanup devices, which may or may not be required depending on quality of fuel, plant location, and government regulations.

Table 10.2. Unit capital cost: 4-year construction period.

Expenditure Year	Base-Cost Estimate	Years of Inflation	Inflated Cost at 6%/year	Years of IDC	IDC Cost at 10%	Total Cost
(1)	(2)	(3)	(4)	(5)	(6)	(7)
4	17.87	0.5	18.40	3.5	6.44	24.84
5	41.69	1.5	45.49	2.5	11.37	56.86
6	41.69	2.5	48.22	1.5	7.23	55.45
7	17.87	3.5	21.91	0.5	1.10	23.01
Year 8 Totals	119.12		134.02		26.14	160.16

Moving in the other direction, i.e. toward the electrical system, the costs of the generator step-up transformer, the high-voltage switchyard, and even transmission lines may or may not be included in the numerator of a unit-cost per kW quotation.

There is also the question of whether interest during construction is included in the numerator.

Finally, and most easily overlooked, is the year of installation. In an inflationary economy, costs quoted as of different years are meaningless for comparison.

Unit Output Designation. The denominator of the $/kW ratio offers nearly as many vagaries as the numerator. The usual value of kW is the net unit output as shown in Fig. 10.1, although the gross, or terminal, output is sometimes used, and occasionally the output at the high-voltage terminals of the step-up transformer. But all of these output designations depend on what is stated to be the output of the steam turbine-generator. The nameplate may give an output rating based on a nominal exhaust pressure quite different from that obtainable at the site; and the latter varies with the season. Output available at overpressure is greater than that at rated pressures; and increased output may be obtained from steam-flow margins designed into boiler and turbine. While various utilities and power pools have standardized the conditions under which a 'maximum dependable capacity' may be defined, not all these standards are alike; and the rating conditions specified for system operation need not apply when quoting plant costs in $/kW.

In the case of gas turbines, it is common to designate two output ratings—a *base* or continuous rating, and a *peak* or short-time rating—which depend on turbine inlet temperature.

Considering all of the above variables of cost and output definitions, it would not be difficult to find a two-to-one variation in $/kW plant cost quotations for two ostensibly identical units. Although some definitions of cost and output seem more reasonable than others, there is no basis upon which to establish 'correct' definitions. It is therefore necessary to be careful, complete, and consistent in defining the plant costs used in generation economic studies.

Plant Cost Economy of Scale

As in the case of O&M costs, it is not uncommon to express the economy of scale of plant cost per kW in exponential form:

$$D = D_0(C_0/C)^x \qquad (10.8)$$

where D = Plant cost of new unit, $/kW
D_0 = Plant cost of base unit, $/kW
C = Rating of new unit, kW
C_0 = Rating of base unit, kW
x = characteristic exponent

Equation (10.8) is identical to eqn (10.5) except for definition of variables. The D-factor may also be used with reference to plant costs, in which case eqn (10.7) applies. While the exponential expression for economy of scale is a useful device for general understandings and for certain kinds of conceptual generation studies, it should be recognized that an actual predictive plot of unit cost as a function of unit size would be extremely difficult to obtain; and if obtained, the D-factor would almost certainly not be constant over a large range of unit sizes. A typical value of D-factor for plant cost is 0.2, with small units ranging higher, and large units lower.

Incremental Plant Costs

It is frequently necessary in generation economic studies to have some idea of the incremental cost of plant capacity as a measure of the value of a small change in design output. This could come about, for example, from an alternate, more efficient design of boiler feed-pump drive that would reduce auxiliary power requirements, hence increase unit net output slightly.

Referring to eqn (10.8), the total plant cost, DC, in dollars, (not \$/kW) is obtained by multiplying by C:

$$DC = D_0 C_0^x C^{(1-x)}. \tag{10.9}$$

The incremental plant cost, D_i, is the slope of this total cost curve, which may be obtained by differentiating with respect to C:

$$\frac{d(DC)}{dC} = D_i = D_0 C_0^x (1 - x) C^{-x}; \tag{10.10}$$

$$D_i = (1 - x) D_0 (C_0/C)^x, \tag{10.11}$$

and, substituting from eqn (10.8),

$$D_i = (1 - x) D. \tag{10.12}$$

For a D-factor of 0.1, eqn (10.6) gives $x = 0.152$. Hence, for this example, $D_i = 0.848\,D$. This means that the cost of an incremental change in output rating is estimated to be 848 \$/kW for a plant whose base cost is 1000 \$/kW.

11
Total System Analysis

As noted in Chapter 6, there are many cases wherein comparisons of alternate generating units may be made using a 'direct unit' analysis, i.e. one without reference to existing or future system generation. Such a comparison involves many assumptions, some direct, some indirect; some expressed, some tacit. When these assumptions are known and understood, and the degree of their approximation is acceptably small, the direct unit analysis can produce valid comparisons. Otherwise, absurdly incorrect results may be obtained.

The advocacy of a generation economic study is always to the result of lowest total cost of electricity as seen by the consumer, i.e. lowest total *system* revenue requirements. There is no validity to an analysis based on the advocacy of a particular generating unit or class of generating units. Hence, when a direct unit analysis is made, one says, in effect, 'I can safely approximate the effect on total system cost of these alternates by comparing their costs alone.' But to make such a statement requires a knowledge of total system cost methods and the varying impacts of alternate generating units on system operation and costs. And this understanding will frequently lead to the conclusion that a direct unit analysis will not suffice.

This chapter will discuss total system analysis procedures. A later chapter will consider the cases in which approximations may be made to permit direct unit analysis.

ANALYSIS PROCEDURE

The essence of total system analysis is simulation of system operation—with respect to both reliability and economy of electric power supply. The simulation is carried out over a period of time which is estimated to include most of the economic impacts of the alternates being studied. One way of defining an adequate length of study is that which will produce, among alternatives, differences in present worth of final-year costs which are small compared to differences in present worth of costs for the total study period. This requirement is usually met by a study of no more than twenty years' length. The simulation of future system operation is repeated for each alternate case, the present worth of the total system cost of each simulation being the basis of comparison.

It might be argued that a decision, for example, to install this or that piece of equipment today based on a study which requires assumptions about conditions twenty years hence is not realistic: no one can predict the future. But it is impossible to escape making assumptions about the long-range future when considering equipment of long-range life. If one thinks to avoid the uncertainty of future conditions by an economic study based on today's conditions only, he is in reality making the assumption that the future will be the same as today— probably the worst assumption that could be made. So assumptions regarding future conditions are necessary; but in total system analysis they are clear, identified, unequivocal assumptions. The 20-year study is not a prediction of

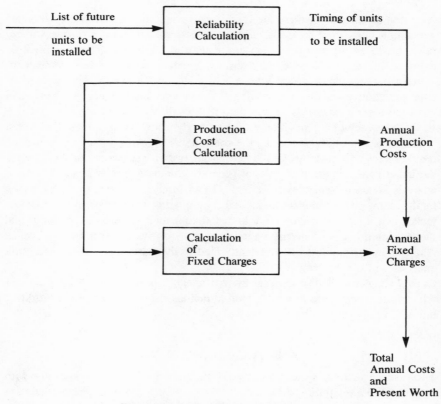

Fig. 11.1. Total system analysis procedure.

the future, but an answer to the question, 'What if these were the future conditions, and I made a certain decision regarding generation?' It should also be noted that a 20-year study is not for the purpose of establishing twenty years' worth of economic decisions: *it is to assist in making a current decision using the insight obtained by considering the future*.

Figure 11.1 is a flow diagram of the total system analysis process. Alternate cases to be studied are defined by the types and sizes of proposed generating units, listed in the sequences in which they are to be added. The reliability calculation then determines the timing of additions, as required to maintain a stipulated reliability, considering the magnitude of the load for each year of the system expansion.

With the pattern of unit additions established, the production-cost calculation determines how the total generating system (original plus added units) should be operated for adequate reliability and maximum economy, calculating costs of fuel and operation and maintenance as it proceeds through each year of the study.

In the third block of Fig. 11.1, the fixed charges are calculated for each year as the product of each unit's capital-cost and fixed-charge rate.

The sum of production costs and fixed charges is the total system cost of the expansion case defined by the original list of future units. Alternate cases having a different unit or units included in the list are analyzed in the same way. In order to compare the cases, which in all likelihood will have varying differences in annual total costs, it is necessary to take the present worth of each nonuniform series of annual costs. The economic choice is the expansion case which has the lowest total present worth of annual costs.

Each of the procedures of Fig. 11.1 is described in more detail below.

RELIABILITY CALCULATION

The reliability calculation is ordinarily a probabilistic one using the LOLP or other similar method. It is possible, however, to establish the time schedule for addition of new units by using a simple reserve criterion, and this is still the practice in some places. This criterion is, 'Add a new unit when the peak annual load for a future year will be such as to produce, with existing capacity, an installed reserve that is less than X percent.' This procedure is many times like 'blind flying.' The purpose of adding new capacity is to maintain system reliability as the load grows, while avoiding the high costs of overbuilding the capacity. The 'percent reserve' method of system expansion offers no real quantitative assurance that either of these purposes has been achieved.

Expansion by Reserve Criterion

To illustrate the problem, consider the expansion of a system with 1200 MW of existing capacity which is considered reliable in serving a peak load of 1000 MW; i.e. the reserve policy is 20%. The largest and most recently added units of this system each have 100 MW capacity and a forced-outage rate (R_f) of 5%. The effects of expanding this system with units of varying size and forced-outage rate can be seen by calculating the reserve required to maintain a constant LOLP as the system grows. This could be done by a full-scale LOLP calculation using capacity models and load models; but it can also be done, although approximately, by using the characteristic slope M as defined in Chapter 9. For this example, the latter method will suffice.

The first step is to estimate the value of M of the existing system to be 5% of the capacity, or 60 MW. The reliability of the existing system is defined as satisfactory for a load of 1000 MW, which means that the LOLP (if it were calculated) would be equal to some acceptable criterion, which in turn means that the *system* effective capacity is 1000 MW. It is not necessary to know the value of LOLP because, in this example, the only purpose is to expand the capacity of the system and find its effective capacity maintaining the same LOLP, whatever it was to begin with. And that is what the effective capacity equation (9.8) does.

For the first case, assume that the expansion continues with 100-MW units of $R_f = 0.05$. Table 11.1 illustrates the procedure. The first line shows the capacity, system effective capacity, and reserve of the original system. The effective capacity, L, of the first added unit is calculated using eqn (9.8) to be:

$$L = 100 - 60 \ln(1 - 0.05 + 0.05e^{1.667}) = 88.3.$$

The second line may now be completed: system effective capacity is 1000 + 88.3 = 1088.3; reserve is (1300 − 1088.3)/1088.3 = 0.194.

The value of M must be adjusted using eqn (9.9):

$$M_2 = 60 \times 1300 \times 0.194/(1200 \times 0.2) = 63.1,$$

which is the value to be used for the calculations of the third line.

This process is continued to complete the table, and the results are plotted as the lowest curve of Fig. 11.2. The required reserve for constant LOLP

Table 11.1. Reserve required for 100 MW units ($R_f = 0.05$).

Unit Added MW	System Capacity MW	M^* MW	Unit L MW	System L MW	System Reserve p.u.
—	1200	—		1000	0.200
100	1300	60	88.3	1088.3	0.194
100	1400	63.1	88.8	1177.1	0.189
100	1500	66.3	89.3	1266.4	0.184
100	1600	69.3	89.6	1356.0	0.180
100	1700	71.9	89.9	1445.9	0.176
100	1800	74.7	90.2	1536.1	0.172
100	1900	77.3	90.4	1626.5	0.168
100	2000	79.7	90.6	1717.1	0.165
100	2100	82.3	90.8	1807.9	0.162

* Before unit addition

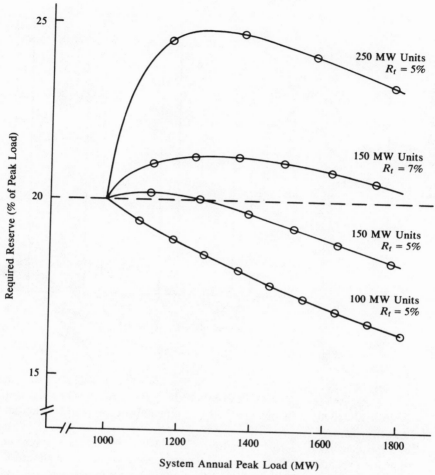

Fig. 11.2. Reserve effect of unit size and forced-outage rate.

declines rather sharply when more of these 100-MW units are added. If the original 20% reserve criterion were to be used to expand this system, serious overbuilding would result. Note that the abscissa of Fig. 11.2 is labeled 'system peak load,' which is identical to system effective capacity when LOLP remains constant.

A similar calculation using 150-MW units, still with $R_f = 5\%$, shows the required reserve rising above 20% for the first added unit, then declining, as shown by the second curve of Fig. 11.2. A 20% criterion here would not be bad for a few years.

The third curve of Fig. 11.2 assumes a shift to a different kind of 150-MW unit with a higher forced-outage rate—7%. The required reserve rises well above 20% and stays there during a near-doubling of the system load.

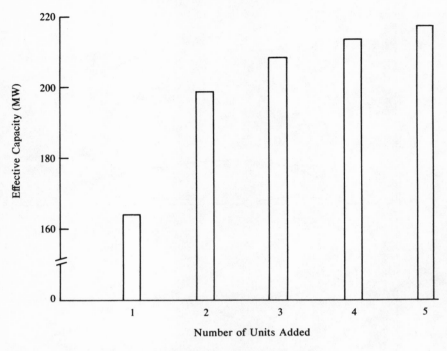

Fig. 11.3. Effective capacity of 250-MW units.

If, finally, the system is 'shocked' by adding units two-and-a-half times the size of the largest existing units, (250 MW), the reserve requirement jumps to nearly 25%, although, as in the other cases, it ultimately declines with saturation of these large units.

The first conclusion to be drawn from Fig. 11.2 is that a percent reserve criterion for expanding a system can produce adequate reliability without excessive capacity only by chance. The second is that a unit of a given size and forced-outage rate tends to require less system reserve as more units are added. Another way of describing this is to say that the effective capacity of each successive identical unit increases. Figure 11.3 shows this effect for the 250-MW units in the postulated system.

Expansion by LOLP Calculation

The approximate method of the previous examples is not really suitable for serious system design calculation of LOLP. A computer program, based on the steps summarized in Chapter 9 and described in the references of that chapter, should be used. Assuming appropriate load and capacity models, the LOLP is calculated to be 0.1 days per year (d/y) for the system of the previous example in year 1, before any capacity additions. This LOLP will be taken as the design, or maximum allowable, value. It is further assumed that the growth in annual peak load is at the rate of 6% per year. A list of future units is selected in which three 150-MW units are to be added, followed by two 250-MW units, all with a 5% forced-outage rate.

Table 11.2 gives the results of the LOLP calculations. In year 2, the LOLP, using the original 1200-MW system is 0.272 d/y, which is above the 0.1 d/y design point. The first of the 150-MW units is added to the system, and a new LOLP calculation gives LOLP = 0.039. This is satisfactory; so the calculation proceeds to year 3, with a peak load of 1124 MW. At this load, the 1350-MW system has a LOLP of exactly 0.100, so no unit need be added in year 3. The process continues, requiring unit additions in years 4 and 5. The system holds in year 6; but when an addition is required in year 7, a shift to the 250-MW size is made, according to the original plan.

Although the only LOLP calculations required to be made are those of Table 11.2, it is illuminating to calculate a few additional points to permit plotting the characteristic curves given in Fig. 11.4. Here one can see the increasing M as the system expands, and can note the increasing effective capacity of the units as measured by the horizontal distance between curves. Note that in contrast to Fig. 11.3, where the first 250-MW unit had an effective capacity of 163 MW, the first one in Fig. 11.4 has an effective capacity of about 190 MW. It is more effective because the system had the opportunity to grow through the prior addition of three 150-MW units.

Table 11.2 represents a schedule of unit additions for the expansion of the system that will provide a future LOLP no greater than 0.1 d/y. The next step is to promulgate other lists, having units of different sizes and forced-outage rates, and establish required timing for them as well. Each such schedule, or pattern, becomes an alternate case whose costs must now be determined.

Table 11.2. System expansion by LOLP.

Year	Peak Load MW	Added Units MW	System Capacity MW	LOLP d/y
1	1000	—	1200	0.100
2	1060	—	1200	0.272
	1060	(1) 150	1350	0.039
3	1124	—	1350	0.100
4	1191	—	1350	0.270
	1191	(1) 150	1500	0.045
5	1262	—	1500	0.118
	1262	(1) 150	1650	0.024
6	1338	—	1650	0.060
7	1418	—	1650	0.162
	1418	(1) 250	1900	0.021
8	1504	—	1900	0.051
9	1594	—	1900	0.125
	1594	(1) 250	2150	0.020
10	1690	—	2150	0.046

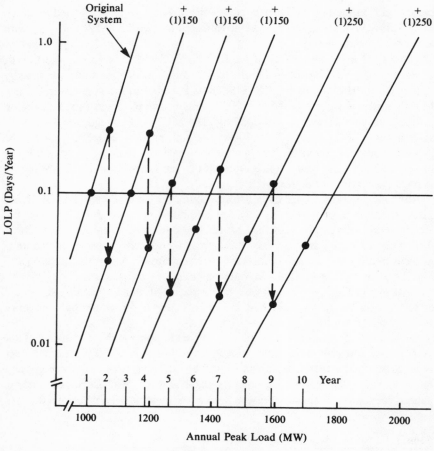

Fig. 11.4. System expansion to LOLP = 0.1.

PRODUCTION–COST CALCULATION

The beauty of total system cost analysis is primarily the beauty of production costing. It is here that the role of each alternate generating unit is revealed—by the simple expedient of letting it 'operate' on the utility system for life, and recording its output and its costs. It operates, in conjunction with every other system generating unit, according to the system operating procedures outlined in Chapter 8: maintenance scheduling, provision for operating reserve, commitment, and economic dispatch. Its operation is determined, hour by hour, year by year, by the changing circumstances of system load and system generation.

Like probability analysis, such detailed simulation was not possible until the introduction of digital computers. The earliest production-costing simulation programs (Galloway, Kirchmayer, Marsh, and Mellor, 1960) allowed, for the first time, the realistic evaluation of then nonstandard forms of generation: nuclear and peaking gas turbines. Further development permitted simulation of pumped-storage hydro dispatch (Galloway, Landes, and Marsh, 1964) and the stochastic recognition of forced outages (Baleriaux, Jamoulle, and de Guertechin, 1967). A paper presented at the Nuclear Utilities Methods Symposium gives useful details of production-costing simulation (Marsh, Moisan, and Murrell, 1974).

Figure 11.5 is a typical logic diagram for a production-costing simulation. The data required for each generating unit of the initial system and of the planned future additions are the same as those required to operate a real system: the required scheduled-maintenance time, the minimum and maximum operating output, the heat rates at these points, the incremental heat rates over the loading range, the fuel price, the operation and maintenance costs, and the start-up costs.

The operating rules include the required spinning reserve, 'rules of thumb' regarding minimum unit operating or shutdown times, and, if appropriate, specifications regarding minimum storage-reservoir levels.

Load data consist of a chronological listing of hourly loads for each year of the study. Frequently, this 'load model' is prepared in per unit form: loads are given as a fraction of the peak load for each year, and the model may be identical for all years. It is then necessary only to specify the peak load for each year to obtain the actual hourly loads for all years. These absolute load values are then augmented or diminished to simulate the effects of known power sales contracts or purchase contracts and the operation of existing or future planned hydroelectric generation.

Any of these modifications may be made by schedules of additions or subtractions to hourly loads. In addition, the economic operation of hydro, which incorporates significant storage capability, may be simulated by a simple 'peak shaving' algorithm in which the monthly energy output is specified, together with minimum and maximum power outputs. The hydro is then scheduled, within these constraints, to operate at times of the day that will reduce, as much as possible, the magnitude of the daily load to be served by the thermal generation of the system. This tends to minimize fuel cost because the highest-cost generation is ordinarily reserved for the shortest-duration peak loads.

With the generation and load characteristics and operating rules all specified, the production-costing process enters the first year of the study. If any thermal units are to be added, their data are incorporated with that of the original system. Referring again to Fig. 11.5, the first step is to schedule maintenance for the year as described in Chapter 8 and Fig. 8.1. The 'maintenance intervals'—or periods during which specific units are considered to be out of service—may be of one to four weeks in duration, depending on the degree of detail possible or desired. A larger number of maintenance intervals tends to increase calculational time, because the loads within a maintenance interval may be made repetitive so that not all hours need be calculated.

The production-costing simulation for each interval begins with the devel-

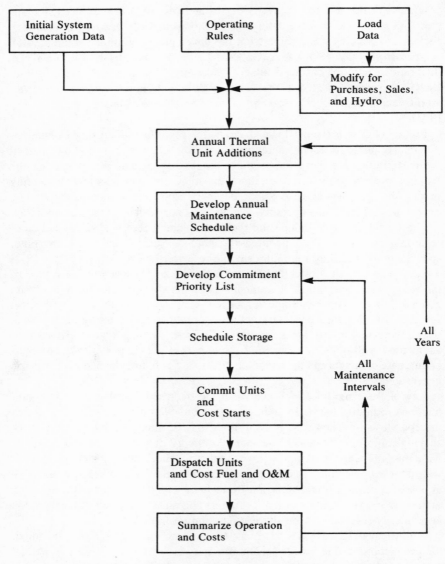

Fig. 11.5. Logic diagram for typical production-costing program.

opment of a priority, or merit, list of generating units which determines the order in which they will be committed. This provides an indication of the fuel-cost levels at which various magnitudes of hourly loads are to be served, and permits the development of an economic schedule for operation of storage plants, if they exist. The procedure is to compare the off-peak cost of charging storage with the on-peak cost of thermal generation. If, considering the storage conversion efficiency and storage capacity constraint, it is possible and economic to operate the storage plant, modification of the hourly loads is accordingly made.

With the scheduling complete for purchases, sales, hydro, and storage plant operation, the thermal units are committed to meet spinning reserve requirements and dispatched to equal incremental costs for each hour of the maintenance interval.

This process must be carried out for all maintenance intervals in the year, because they will have differing complements of available generating units and different hourly loads. At the end of the year, the loads will be increased (and perhaps changed in other respects), new units may be added and old ones retired, and the production-costing procedure repeated for the succeeding year. This of course continues, with annual changes in fuel and operation and maintenance costs as may be specified, for all of the years of the study.

A summary of the production-costing calculation gives not only costs, but operating information for each unit, including number of starts, hours committed, capacity factor, average heat rate, maintenance outages, and fuel consumption.

CALCULATION OF FIXED CHARGES

The usual procedure is to ignore the fixed charges on generating units that are in existence in the year before the study begins because they are common to all cases. Any of these units that may be retired under normal circumstances during the years of the study will be retired in all alternate cases, so the fact that their fixed charges cease will also be common to all cases. However, if the purpose of the study is to consider the question of whether or not to retire a unit, special handling of its fixed charges is necessary. This case will be considered in the next chapter.

The annual fixed charges of each added unit are, of course, the fixed-charge rate multiplied by the unit capital cost as of the installation date. The fixed-charge rate may vary slightly among alternate types of generating units because of different estimated lives, different income or other tax treatment, or different insurance costs. It is simplest, and most common, to use the level fixed-charge rate for all added units, rather than the actual yearly values. This, however, constitutes an approximation whose significance will now be considered.

Level versus Actual Annual Fixed Charges

As examples, Fig. 11.6 gives actual yearly and level fixed-charge rates calculated for a plant of 30-year life under alternate financial and income tax conditions which are listed in Table 11.3. The level values of Fig. 11.6 are, by definition, the values which over a 30-year period have the same present worth as the actual yearly values. However, if the present worth of the level value is taken for a shorter period, it will not be equal to the present worth of the actual values for the shorter period.

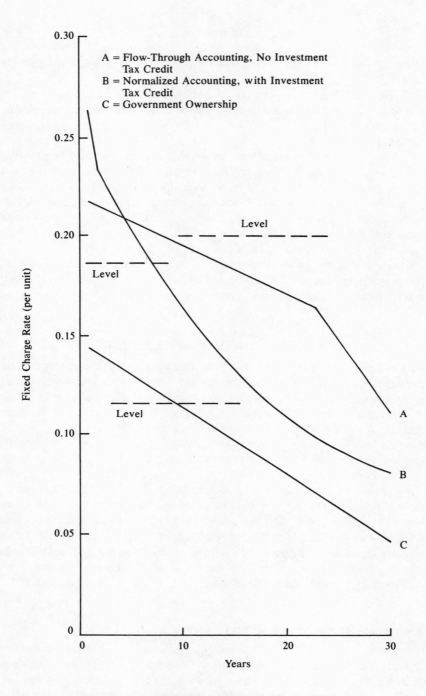

Fig. 11.6. Actual yearly and level fixed-charge rates.

Table 11.3. Basis of fixed-charge rates of Figure 11.6.

	Curve A	Curve B	Curve C
Book life, years	30	30	30
Book depreciation method	SL	SL	SL
MAR, (and discount rate) p.u.	0.12	0.12	0.1
Debt Ratio, p.u.	0.5	0.5	1.0
Bond Interest rate, p.u.	0.1	0.1	0.1
Tax Life, years	22	22	—
Tax Depreciation Method	SYD	SYD	—
Tax Rate, p.u.	0.48	0.48	
Investment Tax Credit, p.u.	—	0.1	—
Tax Accounting Method	Flow Through	Normalize (30 yr.)	—
Ad Valorem Taxes and Insurance, p.u.	0.05	0.05	0.01
Total level fixed-charge rate	0.200	0.186	0.116

To illustrate this point, consider a 20-year generation study where identical units of equal capital cost are added each year. Using the fixed-charge rate of Curve B of Fig. 11.6, the present worth of 20 years' *level fixed charges* for the unit installed in year 1 is:

$$P_L = P' \times \text{fcr}/(\text{CRF})_{20,0.12},$$

where P_L = Present worth of level fixed charges.

P' = Investment (assumed = 100)

fcr = 0.186 (30-year level value)

$(\text{CRF})_{20,0.12} = 0.134.$

Thus: $P_L = 100 \times 0.186/0.134$

$= 138.8.$

If the present worth (P_A) of the first 20 years of the *actual annual* fixed-charge rates of Curve B, Fig. 11.6, is calculated year-by-year, it is:

$$P_A = 143.6,$$

which is larger than P_L, as would be expected. The error in using the 30-year level value for a study period of only 20 years is about 3.3%.

This comparison is shown conceptually as unit no. 1 in Fig. 11.7.

Consider the tenth unit, added in the tenth year. Its error is greater: about 12%. And the unit added in the last year of the study would use a level fixed-charge rate of 0.186, when its actual first-year value is 0.262—an error of nearly 30%.

But these are only single units. In a 20-year study, what is desired is the present worth of the fixed charges of the complete series of 20 units, one added each year. This is obtained by using a tabular calculation and summing the products of investment, fixed-charge rate, and single payment present-worth factor for each year. Since the units with the greatest error occur latest in time,

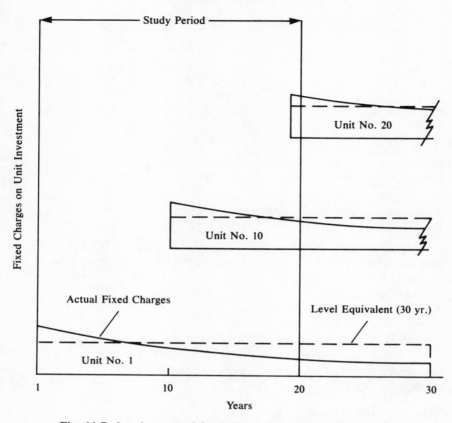

Fig. 11.7. Level vs. actual fixed charges for a 20-year study period.

their errors will be discounted most. The calculation shows the present worth using the level fixed-charge rate to be 975.3; using the actual yearly values, 1059.6. The error in total present worth is about 8%.

Finally, a more realistic case should be considered—one where the investments are growing each year, due partly to physical growth of the generating capacity, and partly to monetary inflation. If 6% growth is assumed for each component (a compound rate of 12.36% per year), and the present worth of fixed charges is recalculated using level and actual yearly values, the results are:

$$P_{\mathrm{L}} = 1988.9;$$
$$P_{\mathrm{A}} = 2232.5.$$

The present worth of fixed charges using the level value is about 11% low.

The example used—Curve B of Fig. 11.6—produces the greatest error of the three, because its slope is steepest. A calculation of the same growth case using Curve A gives only a 4% error; and Curve C would no doubt be close to this. In considering whether to use the actual or level fixed-charge rate in a system study, one should take into account the calculational complexities, as well as the fact that the error introduced by level fixed-charge rates is an *absolute* one, and that it will be in the same direction for all alternate cases. The magnitude of error in the *difference* in present worth of all costs between alternate expansion cases will many times be negligible.

FINANCIAL SIMULATION

While the Revenue Requirements method, using fixed-charge rates, is widely accepted as a means for determining the economic choice among alternate facilities, it cannot provide the complete basis for decision. There are, of course, noneconomic factors (political, for example)—but aside from these is the fact that the fixed-charge rate wraps up within a single number all of the real considerations of capital availability, cash flow, and earnings, in a way which, while theoretically correct, may not be completely satisfying. It in some ways seems to be saying, 'Trust in me, and in the long run you'll come out ahead.'

But when? —and how? The answers to these questions may be obtained by the process of financial simulation, which is to the fixed-charge rate what detailed production-cost simulation is to the simple mills per kWh calculation of unit fuel cost. It is an outgrowth of what is sometimes called a 'book study.' After the engineering economic studies are complete, and the economic choice identified, a utility's financial managers are interested in the near-term effects on financing requirements, cash flow (cash needs), revenue requirements (rate changes), and, of course, earnings. The book study is a projection of the utility's accounting system for a period of five to ten years. It produces estimated income statements, cash reports, and balance sheets for these future years, from which the desired information may be obtained.

Such a study is important because it may show, for example, that the preferred plan, based on long-range economics, has a short-term requirement for large capital investment which is not propitious in the current state of the financial markets. Or it may have a short-range deleterious effect on earnings which, in the existing financial condition of the utility, would not be strategically wise. So the book study adds further pragmatism to the economic study.

Financial simulation is an extension and automation of the book study using straightforward computer simulation to solve the real-time accounting equation given in Chapter 5 [eqn (5.1)] for the complete period of the economic study. As such, it provides a substitute for the fixed-charge rate and involves a reverse-logic procedure: it begins with revenues and calculates return.

One of the added complexities of financial simulation is that, to be at all realistic, it must encompass all of the assets and operations of the concern, not just the generation portion. Usually, however, the capital investment and operating and maintenance costs of the distribution, transmission, and other plant additions through the period of the study may be roughly approximated without a great deal of study of these areas, so long as they are common to all generation alternate cases to be studied. Where it is known that the transmission requirements of one generation plan are markedly different from those of another, then the transmission investments should be accurately included, just as they should be in a Revenue Requirements study.

Estimating future revenues is also necessary, but this need not be very difficult if utility rates are based on an allowable overall return on total investment—because in financial simulation, as noted above, one is dealing with the total assets of the utility.

Inputs to a typical financial simulation are:

Beginning Balance Sheet
Details of Construction Work in Progress
Annual Capital Expenditures for Generation
Annual Generation Production Expense
Annual Capital Expenditures for Other Plant
Annual Expense for Other Plant
Annual Energy Sales
Rules for Rate Regulation
Taxation Rules
Financing Policies
Interest Rates
Estimated Price/Earnings Ratio for Common Stock
Accounting Rules
Dividend Policy
Inflation Rates

The output of the calculation consists of the usual financial statements for each year of the study: operating statement, statement of source and disposition of funds, and balance sheet. An early example of a financial simulation program is described by Carlin, Lyons, et al. (1969).

CRITERIA OF CHOICE

The total system analysis procedure consists of establishing alternate patterns of generation addition to reliably serve projected future loads, then calculating total system production costs for each alternate. To these are added the fixed charges of the capital investments for added generating capacity, giving total annual revenue requirements. The present worth of total revenue requirements is the criterion of economic choice.

If, in addition to the economic analysis, a financial simulation is desired, the same production-cost calculations are made. But the investments, instead of being converted to annual fixed charges, are expressed as actual annual capital expenditures, which, with the annual production expenses, become the basis of the financial simulation. The resulting annual financial statements provide no clear-cut criterion of choice, and they are not intended to.

A utility manager, in considering a decision with respect to generation capacity, must assess many factors, political and societal as well as economic and financial. Although he may be able to identify the one 'economic choice,' his decision may very well be otherwise, as he balances all factors against the varied objectives of his organization. This fact diminishes neither the value nor the importance of economic and financial studies, if for no other reason than that *they provide indispensable measures of the cost of concession to other, noneconomic, factors.*

12
Problems in Total System Analysis

There are a variety of problems in generation economics whose solutions require the use of total system analysis. They range from the straightforward application of conventional forms of generation to an expanding system to considerations of unit retirement. Some of these problems will be discussed in this chapter.

Before proceeding, however, it will again be desirable to differentiate among the operations performed in making a generation study. There are those of designing the study, selecting the economic methodology, gathering data, calculating, analyzing results, drawing conclusions, and presenting them. In total system analysis, particularly, the calculational process is so large—with probability analysis, and production-cost simulation, and combination computer programs which generate their own optimal system expansions—that it is easy to slight the other operations. Yet here is where the value—and the creativity and the satisfaction—of a generation study lies: in objectively defining the question, establishing theses, designing procedures to prove or disprove them, analyzing results, and presenting conclusions. These operations are not easily defined or explained, but the problem examples that follow may illuminate some of them.

If a system of generating units to serve a specified load could be designed all at one time—'from scratch,' as it were—the problem of selecting the economic sizes and types of units would be far simpler than it actually is. Generating systems are in the process of growing, however, and this means that new units must be selected to be operationally and economically compatible not only with the existing units but with those which will come after. That is the principal reason why long-range system simulation studies are required for unit size and type selection. These choices are not really independent: the economic size for one type of generation may not be the same as for another; but the underlying selection principles may nevertheless be separately discussed.

CHOICE OF UNIT TYPE

'Type' of generating unit is meant specifically to designate the prime mover's energy source and method of conversion, e.g. 'nuclear-steam,' 'fossil-steam.' In the case of 'gas turbine,' the energy source is understood to be oil or gas. 'Hydro' means conventional hydroelectric generation, where the flow of water is converted to electrical energy using hydraulic turbines driving generators.

In addition to this generic-type classification is a grouping of units into what may be called applications, or operating modes. Thus, one speaks of 'base-load' or 'midrange,' or 'peaking' units, the appellations suggesting suitability for use on the corresponding portions of a utility load-duration curve, as shown in Fig. 12.1. While such designations are convenient for some purposes, it is important to recognize that they have meaning only in relation to a specific generating system, and that they have both operational and economic implications.

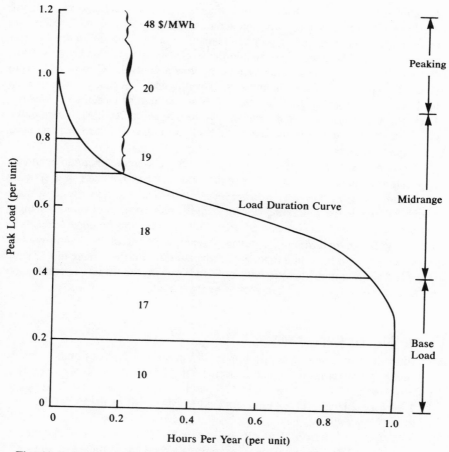

Fig. 12.1. Load-duration curve showing blocks of generating capacity in year 0.

Operational Application Mode

From an *operational* viewpoint, a peaking unit may be one of a number of types of units (gas turbine, hydro, low-pressure fossil-steam) that are physically capable of relatively rapid starting and load changing with minimum risk of damage or excessive maintenance. A base-load unit is one whose inherent physical characteristics make it impossible, or risky, from the standpoint of equipment damage, to sustain such operation. Examples are some nuclear units and most supercritical-pressure fossil-steam units, particularly those operating at high temperature. Midrange units are those types, such as moderate-pressure fossil-steam and combined gas turbine–steam turbine plants, whose operational capabilities lie between those of peaking and base-load units.

Economic Application Mode

Economically, a base-load unit is one whose fuel cost of generation is among the lowest of those making up a generating system, so that under economic commitment and dispatch, it will be operated more or less continuously near its rated output whenever it is available for service and there is load to be served. Its capacity factor may, as a maximum, approach its availability (e.g. 75% to 85%). Peaking units are, economically, those highest-fuel-cost units which are held in reserve or operated only when loads are so high as to demand their use. Their capacity factors are in the range from zero to about 20%. Midrange units, of course, occupy the capacity-factor and fuel-cost ranges between peaking units and base-load units.

The terms 'base load,' 'midrange,' and 'peaking,' when referring to *economic* application modes, are not precisely defined; and, unlike their use in describing *operational* modes, they are, with respect to a particular generating unit, completely relative to the generating system frame of reference. For example, a high-temperature, supercritical-pressure steam unit must always be considered to be a base-load unit, *operationally;* but in a generating system containing nuclear units it might well be a midrange unit, *economically*. Further, since the makeup of a generating system changes with time and growth, the economic application mode of a given unit may change as it becomes older.

Load-Duration Curve Example

To illustrate the economic application modes of various types of units, consider a system of generating units with capacities of oil-fired steam, coal-fired steam, and nuclear units as given in Table 12.1, and intended to serve the load of Fig. 12.1. The cost levels shown are estimated to be typical of the mid-1980s time period. For simplicity, incremental maintenance and heat-rate effects will be ignored; and it is assumed that units will be loaded in accordance with their full-load fuel costs. By plotting each capacity group on the ordinate of Fig. 12.1

Table 12.1. Original system characteristics.

Type	Capacity (in per unit of peak load)	Heat Rate kJ/kWh (Btu/kWh)	Fuel Price $/GJ ($/MBtu)	Fuel Cost $/MWh
Oil-Steam	0.1	11 600 (10 995)	4.15 (4.38)	48
Coal-Steam	0.3	12 100 (11 469)	1.65 (1.74)	20
Coal-Steam	0.1	11 500 (10 900)	1.65 (1.74)	19
Coal-Steam	0.3	10 900 (10 332)	1.65 (1.74)	18
Coal-Steam	0.2	10 300 (9 763)	1.65 (1.74)	17
Nuclear-Steam	0.2	10 530 (9 981)	0.95 (1.00)	10
	1.2			

from bottom to top in increasing fuel-cost order, one may obtain a very rough idea of the relative loading of each type. The total area under the load-duration curve is the per unit energy in the load, and the horizontal bands merely allocate it to the unit-cost groups.

Generation-Duration Curve Example

There are two flaws in this use of the load-duration curve: The base-load units appear to operate continuously all year, and the top 0.2 per unit (p.u.) of the capacity does not operate at all; both of these situations are unlikely, if not impossible. These difficulties may be remedied by using the curve of Fig. 12.2, sometimes called a 'generation-duration curve.' It is shaped so as to permit some operation of the highest-cost units and to limit that of the base-load units, while retaining the same total area, or energy, of the load-duration curve. The shape in this case is arbitrary because the actual shape of a generation-duration curve can be determined only by a complete production-cost simulation which takes into account the hourly load curves and the detailed characteristics of the generating units making up the system. So this curve is not useful in any kind of real generation economic analysis except, perhaps, to display results. However, it is very useful, as used here, to illustrate principles.

Consider now the expansion of the system of Fig. 12.2 for fifteen years, at the end of which time it is assumed that both the system load and the system capacity have doubled. It is taken that all new capacity added is of a slightly more efficient nuclear type having a fuel cost of 9.5 $/MWh. The new generation duration curve is shown in Fig. 12.3. The ordinate, still in per unit of the peak load, now represents twice as many kW; so the original capacity occupies half as much vertical space as formerly, and is forced by the new 9.5 $/MWh capacity

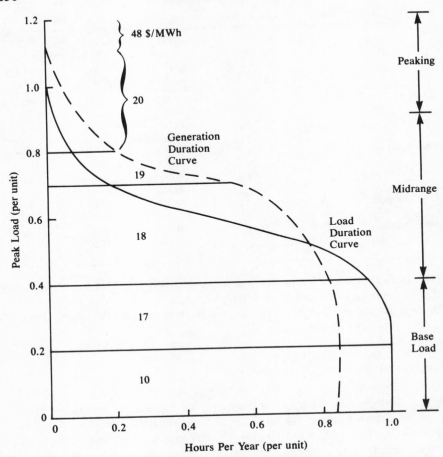

Fig. 12.2. Generation-duration curve showing blocks of generating capacity in year 0.

into the upper part of the curve. The abscissa now represents unit capacity factor if unit operation is always at full-load.

The point illustrated here is that the 10 $/MWh and 17 $/MWh capacity, originally secure in base-load positions, are now shifted to midrange positions. In another fifteen years, they will be peaking units, if the expansion continues by further additions of lower fuel-cost units. There is no obvious problem with this, insofar as the *economics* of system operation is concerned; but there may be a real problem with the *dynamics* of system operation if the specific units making up the 10 $/MWh and 17 $/MWh capacity are not physically capable of the more frequent starts and more rapid load changes implied by their higher position on the curve. This is not merely a theoretical threat; generating systems have actually had to operate less economically, with reduced load on their newest and lowest-cost units, because of high minimum-load requirements and inflexibility of older, higher-cost, erstwhile 'base-load' units. In the extreme, it has been necessary to sell power unprofitably to neighboring utilities at times of the day when there was insufficient system load to support units which could be neither shut down nor reduced in output.

These potential operating difficulties are, of course, the result of continuing to expand a system exclusively with base-load units that are of the newest, most efficient technology, and that are inherently, or designed to be, less flexible than units of other or older technologies. One solution to such difficulties would be to require that all units added to the system be physically capable of peaking operation even though they might initially be economically suitable for base-

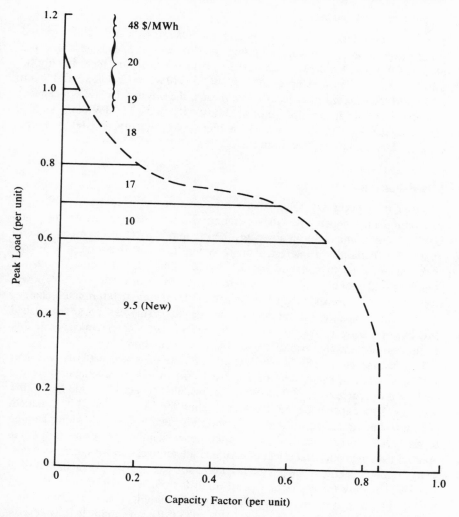

Fig. 12.3. Generation-duration curve showing capacity in year 15 (base-load expansion).

load service. This, of course, would be an extreme requirement and not feasible, although the author believes that much more flexibility of operation could be obtained in units of advanced technology if adequate attention is given in the early design stages.

An alternate solution is to 'let the generation fit the load' (to paraphrase Gilbert and Sullivan). As the base load grows, add base-load units; as the peak load grows, add peaking units. This concept, originally identified by J. B. McClure (Marsh and McClure, 1964), is called a 'mixed-pattern expansion,' as opposed to the 'base-load expansion' of Fig. 12.3.

Mixed-Pattern Operations

The generation-duration curve of Fig. 12.4 illustrates the result of a mixed-pattern expansion for the same system as that of Fig. 12.3. Instead of 0.6 p.u. of added 9.5 $/MWh capacity as in the base-load expansion, there is only 0.3 p.u. The balance is made up of 0.1 p.u. of 35 $/MWh midrange, and 0.2 p.u. of 50 $/MWh peaking capacity. By this means, the original 10 $/MWh capacity remains at an annual capacity factor of almost 85%, the 17 $/MWh only slightly less, and the 19, 20, and 48 $/MWh blocks are actually at slightly higher capacity factors than they were in the original system of Fig. 12.2.

Mixed-Pattern Economics

Whether it is necessary to go this far to control the need for flexibility of generating units depends on the operating characteristics of the existing and potential future units. But in any case, the economic effect of the mixed-pattern approach is certainly of interest. Annual system fuel cost is bound to be higher with the omission of some of the 9.5 $/MWh units. On the other hand, the midrange and peaking units which were added in lieu of them will have lower capital cost. It becomes a matter of balancing the saving of future fixed charges on investment against the future fuel-cost penalty. This can be accomplished only by comparing total system costs, and the fuel-cost penalty can be acceptably calculated only through use of production-cost simulation.

To illustrate the results of total system analysis of mixed patterns, consider a 15-year study of the system of Fig. 12.1, which will be assumed to have a peak load in year zero of 5000 MW and an installed capacity of 6000 MW (20% reserve). Two expansions are developed, using the LOLP method in a manner similar to that described in Chapter 11 and illustrated in Fig. 11.4, but planning to an LOLP of 1.0 d/y. This somewhat-higher-than-normal value is used to approximate the beneficial effect of assumed interconnection with other systems. Two or more interconnected systems may, for example, make a joint LOLP study which shows that a reserve level of 20% provides a desired LOLP of 0.1 for the combined systems. Each utility may then study its own system as though it were isolated, and determine what value of LOLP corresponds to 20% reserve for the combination of loads and units then existing. This LOLP will be higher

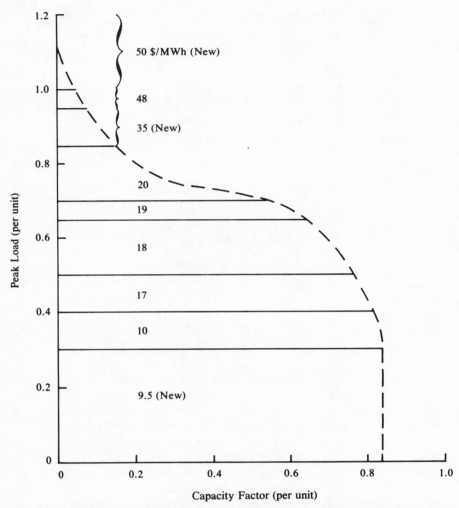

Fig. 12.4. Generation-duration curve showing capacity in year 15 (mixed-pattern expansion).

than 0.1 because each system, isolated, would be less reliable than when interconnected. This higher LOLP, however, is useful as a criterion for independent study of just one utility, while approximating the effect of the interconnection.

The two expansions thus developed are shown in Table 12.2. The base-load expansion, in which nothing but 750-MW nuclear units were added, required 6750 MW of new capacity, giving a final-year reserve of 27.5%. Note that this required reserve, determined from the LOLP calculations, turns out to be different from the 20% of Fig. 12.4, which was simply assumed for the illustration. By contrast, the mixed-pattern expansion requires only 6200 MW of additions to

Table 12.2. System expansions.

| | | | N = Nuclear, | CC = Combined Cycle, | G = Gas Turbine | | | |

| | | Units Added (MW) | |
Year	Peak Load MW	Base-Load Expansion	Mixed-Pattern Expansion
1	5 236	750 N	400 CC, 200 G
2	5 484	750 N	—
3	5 743	—	750 N
4	6 015	750 N	200 G
5	6 300	—	750 N
6	6 598	750 N	200 G
7	6 910	—	400 CC
8	7 236	750 N	200 G
9	7 579	750 N	750 N
10	7 937	—	200 G
11	8 312	750 N	400 G
12	8 706	—	400 CC
13	9 117	750 N	750 N
14	9 548	750 N	200 G
15	10 000	—	400 G
Capacity Added, MW		6 750	6 200
Year 1 Capacity		6 000	6 000
Year 15 Capacity		12 750	12 200
Year 15 Reserve, %		27.5	22

hold the LOLP to 1.0 because more than half the new capacity is in combined-cycle and gas turbine units whose sizes and forced-outage rates are less than those of the base-load expansion. The actual sizes of the gas turbine units would probably be smaller than the 200 MW shown; but with a system as large as this, neither LOLP nor production-cost calculations are distorted by 'lumping' the gas turbines, and the computational time may thus be reduced.

Table 12.3 gives the economic characteristics of the added units. The average incremental heat rate applies between the minimum-load output and the full-load output, and, with the full-load heat rate, defines the input-output curve. Capital, fuel, and O&M costs are all assumed to escalate at 8% per year. The fixed-charge rate is taken as 18%, and the discount rate is 12%.

With these data and corresponding data for the units existing in year zero, production costs for the fifteen years were calculated using a bi-hourly load model and a method similar to that illustrated in Fig. 11.5. The fixed charges on the investment in capacity added were also calculated for each year. These results are tabulated in Table 12.4, together with the present worth as of year 1 of each component and of total system cost.

The mixed-pattern expansion shows a net saving of 1082 M$, which is 9.6% of the base-load-case total cost. Therefore, in seeking a mixture of future generating units that may provide more flexible system operation, there has been found, for these assumptions, not an economic penalty, but a substantial saving.

Table 12.3. Unit economic characteristics (costs as of year 0).

	Nuclear Steam	Combined Cycle	Gas Turbine
Rating, MW	750	400	200
Minimum Load, MW	150	80	2
Full-Load Heat Rate, kJ/kWh	10 000	8 540	12 000
(Btu/kWh)	(9 479)	(8 095)	(11 374)
Avg. Incr. Heat Rate, kJ/kWh	9 750	8 326	8 842
(Btu/kWh)	(9 242)	(7 892)	(8 381)
Fuel Cost, $/GJ	0.95	4.15	4.15
($/MBtu)	(1.00)	(4.38)	(4.38)
O&M Cost			
Fixed—$/kW-yr	5.1	1.8	0.8
Variable—$/MWh	1.3	2.0	3.3
Plant Cost, $/kW	1 100	550	270

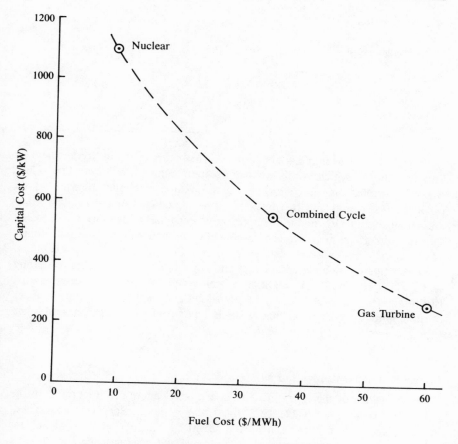

Fig. 12.5. Cost characteristics of expansion units.

Table 12.4. Results of mixed-pattern study.

	Fixed Charges on New Capacity, M$		Production Costs, M$	
Year	Base-Load	Mixed-Pattern	Base-Load	Mixed-Pattern
1	160	53	476	532
2	334	53	490	606
3	334	240	562	623
4	536	254	585	712
5	536	472	672	740
6	771	487	715	849
7	771	555	821	974
8	1046	573	885	1119
9	1343	870	965	1177
10	1343	891	1104	1354
11	1689	936	1218	1561
12	1689	1036	1392	1804
13	2093	1440	1539	1922
14	2529	1468	1720	2224
15	2529	1530	1961	2575
Present Worth	5748	3465	5534	6735

Present Worth of Total System Cost, Base-Load Expansion	11 282 M$
Present Worth of Total System Cost, Mixed-Pattern Expansion	10 200
Mixed-Pattern Net Saving	1 082 M$

This illustrative example is not atypical. The nature of the utility load and its time variations, which result in load-duration curves similar to Fig. 12.1, generally creates an inherent need for a mixture of capital-intensive, low-production-cost units and fuel-intensive, low-capital-cost units to obtain minimum total system cost. In this example, only three types of units were considered for expanding the system: nuclear, combined-cycle, and simple-cycle gas turbine. Their capital costs and fuel costs are plotted in Fig. 12.5. Other types of units, having different combinations of fuel and capital costs (not necessarily falling on the curve of Fig. 12.5), might have been tested, perhaps with better results. But the underlying principle would almost certainly apply: a mixture of types of units is more economical than a single type. And it provides more flexible system operation.

Mixed-Pattern Optimization

The proportions of the types of units in a mixed pattern are important. In the base-load expansion of Table 12.2, 6750 MW of nuclear capacity was added; in the mixed-pattern expansion only 3000 MW. Thus, 3750 MW of nuclear capacity was effectively displaced by midrange and peaking capacity, and this resulted in higher production cost and lower fixed charges. It will be instructive to investigate two additional cases in which different amounts of nuclear capacity were displaced. Table 12.5 defines these and the original two cases and gives comparative results.

In Table 12.5, Mixed Pattern B is the case previously defined, while A and C are patterns with less and more nuclear displacement, respectively. The production-cost penalties and fixed-charges savings of the mixed-pattern cases are all relative to the base-load case. If these penalties and savings are plotted as a function of displaced nuclear capacity, the curves of Fig. 12.6 result. The fixed-charges saving is a roughly linear function of nuclear displacement, as would be expected. The production cost penalty is sharply nonlinear because of the shape of the load-duration curve and the higher fuel costs of the units operating in the upper portion of the duration curve. This effect is apparent from a comparison of Fig. 12.3 with Fig. 12.4. In the base-load expansion, for example, the 19 $/MWh capacity operates at only about 10% capacity factor, while in the mixed-pattern expansion it operates at 65%. This and similar action of other high-cost units is the reason for the rapid increases in production costs when nuclear capacity is displaced. Note that the operating-capacity factors of the new combined-cycle and gas turbine capacity in Fig. 12.4 are quite low and have little effect on system production costs. It is the absence of the nuclear units, forcing increased operation of existing higher-cost units, that is most significant in the production-cost penalty.

The net saving curve of Fig. 12.6 is typical in its shape: the net saving is relatively insensitive to the mix of the units over a fairly broad range. From about 2500 MW to over 4000 MW of displaced capacity, it varies less than 10% from the saving of the optimal 3500-MW displacement. Another characteristic of the curve is its rapid decline to zero and below, once the optimum has been passed.

Optimized Generation Planning

These two characteristics reflect the fundamental mechanism of mixed-pattern economics, which balances investment costs and production costs. The optimal

Table 12.5 Extended mixed-pattern study (year 1 present worth).

Expansion Cases	Base Load	Mixed Pattern A	Mixed Pattern B	Mixed Pattern C
Nuclear Additions, MW	6750	4500	3000	1500
Comb.-Cyc. Additions, MW	—	800	1200	1200
G.T. Additions, MW	—	1200	2000	3300
Total Additions	6750	6500	6200	6000
Nuclear Displacement	—	2250	3750	5250
P.W. Prod. Cost, M$	5534	6032	6735	8463
Prod.-Cost Penalty	—	498	1201	2929
P.W. Fixed Charges, M$	5748	4337	3465	2598
Fixed-Charges Saving	—	1411	2283	3150

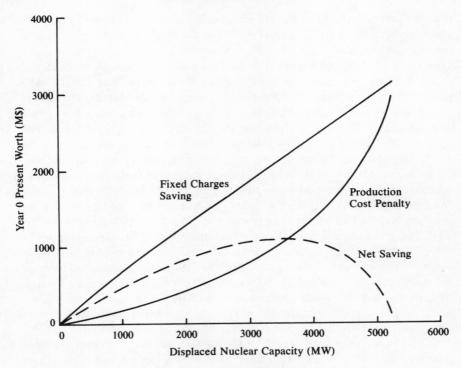

Fig. 12.6. Mixed-pattern costs.

mix in this example was obtained by trying a full range of mix proportions for the 15-year period and plotting the results. It is, however, possible to develop an expansion of near-optimal mix directly, by proceeding one year at a time, trying alternate types of generation, and selecting the one type, or combination of types, that produces lowest total system cost for each year. This approach, incorporating anticipatory logic to recognize future changing conditions, and including LOLP calculations to determine the required amount of various types of generation, is embodied in an *Optimized Generation Planning* (OGP) program, described by Galloway, Marsh, and Miller (1969). Other methods to accomplish similar results are described by Day, Federowicz, and Menge (1973) and by Jenkins and Joy (1974).

These methods permit very rapid analysis and are hence quite valuable in appraising variations in the large number of parameters encountered in generation economic studies.

CHOICE OF UNIT SIZE

The classical concept of unit-size selection is that of finding an optimal balance between the lower capital cost and the higher reserve cost of larger units relative to those of smaller units. These are the obvious considerations, but there are others which may in some cases be nearly as important.

Economy of Scale

One tends to believe, either intuitively, through experience, or from study and understanding of the proportion of the fixed and size-dependent components of the total installed plant cost, that there is some reduction in plant cost per kW of rating as unit size increases. This economy of scale is illustrated in Fig. 12.7, which arbitrarily takes the cost of a 100-MW unit as 1150 $/kW and describes a curve of 10% D-factor (Chapter 10) to 1000 MW. The shape and level of such curves vary considerably with type of unit and with time and place: they must be separately determined for each specific occasion.

Similarly, there is an economy of scale of operation and maintenance costs, illustrated in Fig. 12.8. Its importance in the economics of unit size is less than that of capital cost, but still significant. For example, the difference between the O&M cost for 200- and 400-MW units is $1.61 - 1.29 = 0.32$ $/MWh. At 70% capacity factor, and 18% fixed-charge rate, this may be capitalized (assuming no future inflation):

$$\text{Capitalized O\&M} = 0.32 \times 0.7 \times 8760/(0.18 \times 1000)$$
$$= 10.9 \text{ \$/kW}$$

By contrast, the plant cost difference between these unit sizes is about 100 $/kW.

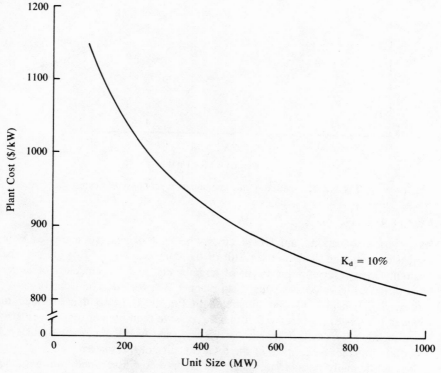

Fig. 12.7. Plant cost economy of scale.

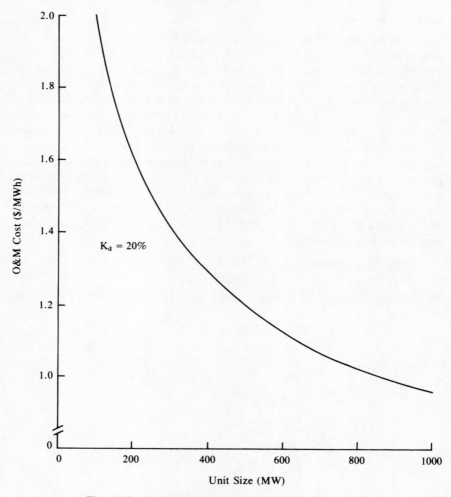

Fig. 12.8. Operation and maintenance economy of scale.

Cost of Reserve

As opposed to capital and O&M costs, the cost of reserve increases with increasing unit size. This is the result of the compounding of two effects, the inherent larger-reserve requirement of larger units, and the tendency of larger units to have higher outage rates, both planned and forced. These factors were discussed in Chapter 11 and illustrated in Fig. 11.2. Also demonstrated in Chapter 11, however, was the fact that the reserve requirement for a given size of unit ultimately declines as successive units are added, i.e. as the unit size becomes a smaller percentage of the total capacity of the system.

It is not actually possible to isolate the reserve cost associated with a single unit or group of units in an expanding system as a single number. This is because it changes with time and mix of unit types. But the principle, at least, may be illustrated. In Fig. 12.9, the plant cost curve of Fig. 12.7 is reproduced, together with curves of estimated reserve cost for two system sizes. (Fuel and O&M costs are neglected.) The sum of plant cost and reserve cost produces totals whose minima occur at different unit sizes: about 350 MW for the original system and about 550 MW for the system of doubled size. It should be emphasized that Fig. 12.9 is wholly conceptual and does not suggest that there is necessarily an economic limit to unit size as systems grow larger.

Other Size-Related Costs

System fuel costs may change significantly with unit-size changes. The question of optimal unit size arises ordinarily only with respect to base-load types whose fuel costs are lower than the system average. To the extent that the larger reserve requirement of larger units is provided by increasing the amount of these same base-load units, there would accrue a system fuel-cost benefit. A simultaneous investigation of optimal unit type, however, might result in some portion of the added reserve being economically supplied as peaking units, in which case it would not be easy to separate the unit-size and unit-type effects on system production cost.

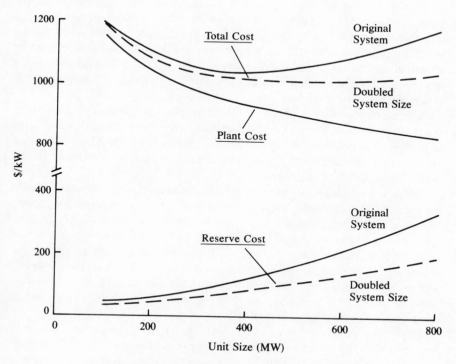

Fig. 12.9. Principles of optimal unit size.

It is conceivable that air-pollution requirements might influence the choice of unit size. For example, postulate a site for a coal-fired plant which is economically desirable because of proximity to loads and availability of low-cost cooling water, but limited to 100 MW in size because of the effect of flue-gas discharge on the desired level of ambient air-pollutants. If another, remote site were available where air pollution would not be limiting, but where water supply were inadequate, then larger units at the remote site could be said to bear the penalty of cooling tower and additional transmission costs. The determination of the significance of these considerations awaits future developments in air-quality control.

Studies of optimal unit size are always complex and frequently unsatisfying. They require numerous system simulation studies, and very careful analysis of results if the true unit-size effects are to be identified. Usually, the most that can be done is to select a unit-size *policy*—a range of economic unit size expressed as a percentage of the growing system capacity. An early example of a study having this result is that reported by Kirchmayer, Mellor, O'Mara, and Stevenson (1955).

THE EFFECTS OF TRANSMISSION

In considering the impact of power transmission on the economic choice of generating-unit type and size, it is convenient (and simplifying) to say that a transmission system has two basic functions: (1) to deliver power under normal operating conditions from the generating units to the load centers; and (2) under abnormal conditions to make the output of any generating unit available as a reserve in the event of the loss of any other unit. The first function is primarily concerned with unit type, the second with unit size.

Different types of units present differing requirements and opportunities for siting, and economic comparisons among them should include the differing costs of requisite transmission. Sometimes this is fairly straightforward, as in the case of a remotely-situated hydroelectric plant, where a simple radial transmission connection is easily identifiable.

Although the locations of fossil or nuclear steam units may be technologically freer than hydro, the legal limitations on land use, the requirements for cooling water and fuel supply, and restrictions on the environmental discharges of these types of units almost always require siting which is also remote from load centers. This implies some amount of dedicated transmission to deliver the output into the bulk transmission system. In a power system of high load density with a large high-voltage transmission network, the amount of transmission allocable to an added generating unit may be only a few dollars per kW; in less dense systems it may be quite significant.

Some types of peaking generation, such as simple-cycle gas turbines, may incur less transmission cost for power delivery than base-load types. Their small unit size permits an electrical location in a lower-voltage part of the system—perhaps at an existing subtransmission substation, for example—and their independence from the need for cooling water and large-scale fuel deliveries tends to enhance the feasibility of location at such sites.

The second function of transmission, i.e. making the system reserve generation available to any point in the system, may be influenced by generating-unit size. When a unit is suddenly lost, other units automatically increase output, and the power flows on transmission lines change accordingly. Voltages and currents may fluctuate widely, and if transmission capacity is insufficient, stability may be threatened. Hence there is the possibility that the selection of a large generating unit would require strengthening of the transmission system, whereas a smaller one would not.

Considerations of transmission-cost effects in the selection of generating-unit sizes and types are not ordinarily overriding. Frequently, the difference in required transmission for alternate generation plans is not a fixed one, but a difference in the timing of the expansion of the transmission system with growth in load. It is important, however, to recognize the interactions between expanding generation and transmission systems by coordination of planning studies. This does not mean that every generation economic study must be accompanied by a complete transmission study, because the economic implications of transmission can frequently be incorporated into the generation study by appropriate additions to capital costs; but enough transmission work must be done to identify and reasonably quantify those implications.

Interconnection of Systems

The interconnection of two or more independent power systems can produce substantial benefits, particularly if it is accompanied by joint planning and operation of the combined systems.

Generation reserve margins may be reduced because the interconnected systems constitute, from a probability viewpoint, a larger base system. This makes the relative size of generating units smaller, and the reserve requirement for a given LOLP less. Alternatively, the benefit could be taken in the economies of larger units, maintaining the same reserve margins. The capacity of the transmission interconnection required to obtain maximum reserve benefit may be determined by probability studies, as first described by Kirchmayer, Mellor, and Simmons (1957).

Interconnections may also produce lower fuel expense, to the extent that a heat-rate or fuel-cost advantage of one power system can be shared with the others.

RETIREMENT OF UNITS

The purpose of most generation studies is to select economic types and sizes of future units, the need for which results from load growth, coupled with the known or assumed retirement of existing units whose useful life will have expired. A schedule of units and their retirement dates is prepared as input to a typical 20-year study, and, as the study progresses, units are dropped from the LOLP and production-cost capacity models as retirements occur. They are thus properly reflected in the system reserve requirements and the production costs. There is no need to consider capital-cost effects if the retirements are common to all alternate cases being studied.

The situation is, of course, different if the question to be studied is whether, or when, to retire a unit. Then, the LOLP and production costs are handled as above, but there will also be a change in the fixed charges of the retired unit if it is retired earlier than the date corresponding to its book depreciation life. After that date, all fixed charges stop, and the retirement versus retention decision is not influenced by the unit's own fixed charges.

When a unit is retired early, before its book depreciation life has expired, an undepreciated balance exists in the plant account, which must be removed by a one-time depreciation charge in the year of retirement. At the same time, the return component of the fixed-charge rate goes to zero. Thus the present worth of total depreciation charges increases, while that of total return decreases, with the result that their sum is the same as though the plant had remained in service to the end of its life. This is exactly true when the discount rate is i, and approximately true for other discount rates. Thus, these components of the fixed-charge rate generally may be neglected: their effect on present worth of revenue requirements is minimal.

Not so with taxes, which cease upon early retirement and represent a reduction in revenue requirements. The present worth of the savings, as of the year of retirement, is:

$$\text{Retirement Tax Savings} = \sum_{y=n_1}^{y=n} \frac{A(y) + T(y)}{(1 + r)^y}, \tag{12.1}$$

where $A(y)$ = annual ad valorem taxes and insurance
   $T(y)$ = annual income tax
   r = discount rate
   n_1 = early retirement year
   n = normal retirement year.

The value of $A(y)$ is frequently equal for all years; so the present worth would be calculated directly using the CRF for the remaining years. $T(y)$ is not level; the values are obtained from the equations for yearly fixed-charge rate, either eqn (5.17) or eqn (5.19). This is quite cumbersome, however, and in many cases a satisfactory approximation is to use the level income tax component of the fixed-charge rate with the appropriate CRF, as with ad valorem taxes.

In any case, the impact on total system costs of the saving in taxes on the retired unit is usually relatively small. More important is the need to advance the installation dates of scheduled new capacity to make up the deficiency as measured by the LOLP calculations. The fixed charges on this new investment are a penalty to early retirement. On the other hand, the replacement capacity will very likely have lower fuel and O&M costs than the retired unit, which is a benefit of early retirement.

The procedure for analyzing early retirement may be summarized as follows:

1. Develop a 20-year expansion schedule with normal retirement.
2. Develop an expansion schedule of equal reliability with early retirement.
3. For each schedule of additions, calculate the present worth of production costs and, for new investment, of fixed charges.
4. Subtract the present worth of saved taxes on the retired unit from the total present worth of the early retirement plan.
5. Select the plan having lowest total present worth.

It may be useful to mention that, in the past, units were seldom retired until the need for major maintenance or replacement of equipment became apparent. One study of U.S. utilities showed an average retirement age of forty-four years for steam units. As limitations on fuel use and plant emissions become more stringent, there may be a trend to earlier retirement of some types of units.

13
Analysis of Storage
and
Renewable Energy Sources

Conventional thermal generation may be considered to operate from an unlimited energy supply, at least to the extent that its fuel inventory is maintained at a level equivalent to several weeks' operation at rated load. Further, the rate of energy input, hence the power output, may be effectively controlled. The so-called renewable energy sources, such as the sun and the wind, have neither of these characteristics: the supply of energy is insufficient to permit continuous operation at maximum output; and if it is to be used, it must be taken at such random times as it is available. The only possible control is to reduce output by wasting input.

Storage devices are not sources of energy—they are actually net users of energy—but for analytical purposes they may be considered as generating units whose energy supply is limited but can be controlled either to increase or decrease output.

The evaluation of these limited-energy forms of generation using total system analysis methods is discussed in this chapter.

ENERGY STORAGE

The electric power industry is not unique in having a capability for continuous production that is not matched by continuous consumption. But it is unusual in that very little use is made of product storage to level out production and thereby reduce the need for production capacity equal to the peak rate of consumption. In other industries, such as automobile manufacturing, for example, the storage is called warehousing; and while it has important functions in overcoming manufacturing and distribution time lags (which are *not* present in electric power production), warehousing also plays an important part in leveling the need for production capacity.

In contrast, however, to other commonly stored products, alternating-current electricity cannot be stored without first converting it to some other form. So the cost of moving it into and out of storage is appreciable, in terms of both product losses and the capital investment required for the conversion apparatus. Significant capital investment is required for the storage reservoir, which must be large enough to assure no interruption in the supply of electricity when demanded by consumers. Unlike other industries, the product 'shipping date' is always *now*.

It is generally true that the capital investment required for storage conversion and storage reservoirs is equal to or greater than that required for at least some kinds of complete production facilities. Hence, for storage systems to be viable, there must be some economic incentive other than that of capital savings. This incentive may sometimes be found in the opportunity to obtain fuel savings in the operation of the generating system. This opportunity exists because of the mixture of old and new and different kinds of generating units on a typical generation system. Because of this, the cost of production varies over a wide range from, for example, 5 $/MWh for nuclear units to 30 $/MWh for peaking gas turbines. While it is not possible to use storage systems to transfer the very-lowest-cost generation from the time of base load to the time of peak load (because, economically, this generation will be running constantly at full-load output all of the time anyway), it may be possible to transfer the cost of some midrange generation to the time of peak with a resulting net saving. This may make the difference between an economic and a noneconomic application of storage systems.

Economic Operation of Storage Systems

In order to understand how this generating system fuel saving can be obtained using storage systems, it is necessary to recognize two categories of storage. Figure 13.1 is a simple diagram of a generating system consisting of several conventional thermal generating units connected to a common ac electrical bus serving a load. In practice, of course, the generating units and the loads are connected to many buses geographically remote from each other but interconnected by transmission lines. From the standpoint of the present discussion of energy flow and economic operation, however, the technology may be adequately explained by this simplification. At the top of the diagram is shown a storage system which may be called *general storage* because its source of energy for charging the storage reservoir is the generating system in general: no one generating unit or energy source may be identified as supplying the stored energy. At the lower part of the diagram is shown a storage system which may be called *dedicated storage* because only energy from the source associated with a particular unit may be stored.

In general storage, the energy conversion apparatus always converts from ac electricity to something else. Examples are pumped-storage hydro and flywheels. In dedicated storage, energy is removed from a generation cycle partway through

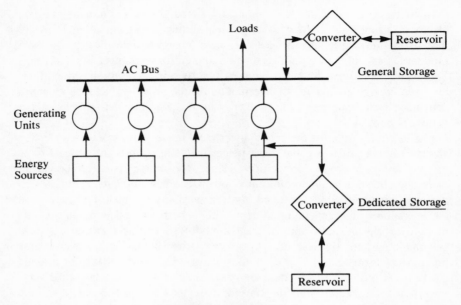

Fig. 13.1. Storage systems.

the conversion from source to ac electricity and either stored directly or converted to a third form and stored. An example of direct storage of an intermediate form of energy is where high-pressure steam from a conventional boiler may be stored in a pressure vessel for use at a later time. Other examples include the storage in oil of the heat in a feedwater heating system in a conventional steam cycle, and the storage of heat in eutectic salts or chemical heat pipes. In these latter examples, energy conversion is required in the charging and discharging of the storage reservoir.

A special category of storage exists in the cases where direct-current electricity is produced from photovoltaic sources or direct conversion methods, such as fuel cells or magnetohydrodynamic channels (MHD). Here, storage may be in the form of storage batteries; but since the inverter, which would be necessary even without storage for converting from dc to ac electricity, may also be used as a rectifier in the opposite direction, the storage batteries are really accessible to the generating system generally. Because of the close physical and technical association of the storage battery with the generating unit, it is natural to think of, or conceive of, this kind of a system as dedicated storage, whereas it is actually operable as general storage.

Operation of General Storage. Once a storage system has been purchased and installed as part of a generating system, its capital costs are 'sunk'; the system may be operated or not depending upon the objectives of the generating system. The prime objective of the generating system is never to fail to serve the consumer demand. At certain times the discharge capacity of the storage reservoir may be essential to meet the peak load. This may or may not represent economic operation of the storage system. At other times, when the discharge capacity is *not* required to meet the peak load, it may still be economical, from a fuel-cost standpoint, to operate the storage system. In theory, if the storage system has been properly designed and applied to the particular generating system involved, it should seldom have to be operated when it is uneconomical.

Figure 13.2 is a stylized daily-load curve for the purpose of illustrating storage system operation. The vertical scale at the left measures the hourly loads in percentage of the peak load for the day. The scale at the right represents, in proportion to the peak load, the capacity of generating units having unit production costs as shown. The bottommost segment, representing about 30% of the peak load, at 5 $/MWh, could represent conventional nuclear generating units, while those above it could correspond to conventional fossil-fired generating units having higher fuel price as measured in $/GJ ($/MBtu) and higher heat rates in kJ/kWh (Btu/kWh). It is apparent that in serving this particular load curve, the 5 $/MWh nuclear units would run continuously, as would the 10 $/MWh fossil units above them. Other, higher-cost units would run for varying times during the day.

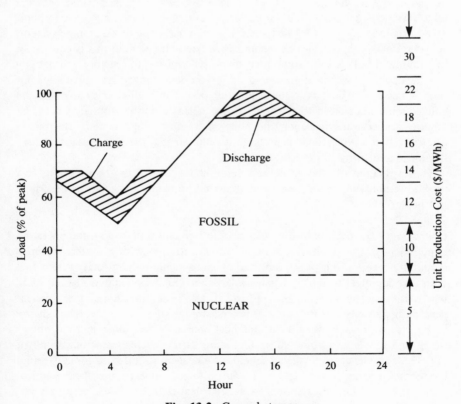

Fig. 13.2. General storage.

The operation of a general storage system is shown by the cross-hatched areas marked 'charge' and 'discharge.' During the charging time the storage system is taking ac electric power from the generation system, which effectively increases the load. During the discharge time the storage system is supplying energy and capacity, effectively decreasing the load 'seen' by the generating system. Referring to the vertical scale at the right, the generating units whose load must be increased in order to supply the charging energy have costs of 12 and 14 $/MWh, averaging about 13. During the discharge cycle, the generating units which otherwise would be operating, but which now may be reduced in load or shut down completely, have production costs of 18 to 22 $/MWh, averaging about 20. There are losses in the conversion of ac electric energy into either dc electric energy or potential hydraulic energy, for example; and there are also losses when the stored energy is reconverted into ac electrical energy. For purposes of analysis, it is convenient and conventional to assign all of the losses to the charging portion of the cycle. This is illustrated in Fig. 13.2 by the charge area for energy being about 40% larger than the discharge area. This corresponds to an overall 'round-trip' efficiency of about 71%.

If the cost of the charging energy is thus 13 $/MWh, then the equivalent cost of the energy in storage is 13/0.71 or 18.3 $/MWh. This, compared with the 20 $/MWh cost of generating the peak load in the absence of a storage system, gives a fuel saving of 1.7 $/MWh resulting from operation of the storage system. At 1000 hours/year discharge time and 18% fixed-charge rate, this is equivalent to a saving of 9.44 $/kW capital investment. Obviously, this saving will not pay for the capital investment in storage reservoir and conversion apparatus, nor does it need to. There is a corresponding saving in capital investment in the conventional generation that would, in the absence of the storage system, be required to serve the peak load now served by the storage system. But this is true only if reservoir capacity is large enough so that the storage system may be considered 'firm on the load curve.'

The evaluation of storage devices requires the use of the total system cost method, employing production simulation and probability analysis as described in Chapter 11.

Operation of Dedicated Storage. Contrary to frequent supposition, the operating requirements of a dedicated storage system, for generating system security (assuredly meeting the peak load) and economy (minimizing total system fuel cost), are identical to those of general storage. This is illustrated in Fig. 13.3, where the nuclear capacity of Fig. 13.2 has been transmuted into nuclear generating capacity incorporating dedicated storage, the cycle of which is shown in Fig. 13.4. This implies a nuclear heat source of the same thermal output rating and the same turbine-generator rating as the nuclear generating unit of Fig. 13.2. However, to this has been added a heat-transfer device for converting the thermal energy in the reactor coolant to thermal energy stored in chemical form or in eutectic salt solution. A second heat-transfer device permits withdrawing heat from storage and making the steam to drive a second turbine-

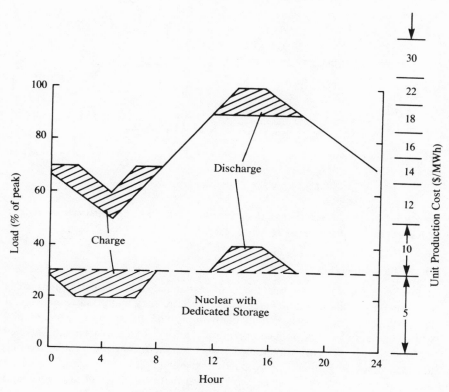

Fig. 13.3. Dedicated storage.

generator having about a third of the rating of the main turbine-generator. Figure 13.4 is typical of several dedicated storage schemes which have been considered.

Referring again to Fig. 13.3, the nuclear unit operates on the charge cycle by diverting part of the reactor steam flow from the main steam turbine-generator to the storage reservoir. At the time of system peak load, the reservoir is discharged, producing power in the smaller turbine-generator. It might appear that such an operation makes the low-cost nuclear energy available to serve the peak load. A study of Fig. 13.3, however, shows that when the nuclear unit has reduced its output to permit charging the heat storage reservoir, the effect is to impose an additional load on the remainder of the generating system so that the same high-cost generating units must go into service during the hours zero to 8, as was the case with the general storage of Fig. 13.2. Similarly, during the hours 13 to 18, the discharge of the storage reservoir permits backing off generation on the 18 and 22 $/MWh units exactly as in Fig. 13.2. The fuel economics are identical because the fuel input to the nuclear/storage unit heat source is constant; and the only fuel consumption that changes with the operation of the storage units is that of the 12 and 14 $/MWh fossil units and the 18 and 22 $/MWh fossil peaking units. *The cost of energy going into storage is always*

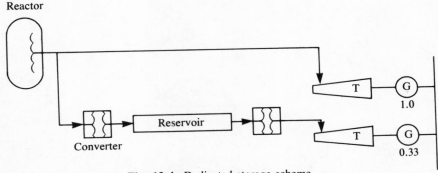

Fig. 13.4. Dedicated storage scheme.

measured by the production cost of the system generating units whose output is increased because energy is being stored.

Other Considerations

It has been shown above that the fuel economics of a storage system are a function only of the overall charge-discharge efficiency and production costs of the existing generating system units that will provide the energy for storage, and whose operation will be reduced or eliminated by storage discharge. The fact that the storage system is integrated with a very efficient low-cost generating unit does not change this. The production-cost examples of Figs. 13.2 and 13.3 were purely illustrative; one can see how the fuel economics of storage would change with a change in the vertical scale of production cost of the generating system's existing units. For example, by looking ahead to some future year and supposing a generating system could be saturated with nuclear units up to 60% or 70% of the peak load, it would be possible to charge the storage at very low nuclear production cost and discharge when relatively high production cost fossil units would otherwise have to operate. This could increase the fuel savings from something under 2 $/MWh to perhaps 6 or 8. Similarly, an increase in overall storage efficiency above the 0.71 assumed in the example would enhance the viability of storage systems.

Aside from the operating economics of storage systems, careful consideration should be given to their ability to assure the peak load. This is largely a function of the amount of storage provided and is best measured by the number of hours of energy available at full discharge rate. The required amount of storage cannot be selected merely on the basis of producing a balanced design of a storage scheme. Nor can it be selected by simple reference to a load curve as in Figs. 13.2 and 13.3. Consideration must be given to generating system emergencies (such as the loss of a major generating unit or heavily loaded incoming transmission line), and this may require several hours more storage than would be dictated by normal economic daily or even weekly operation. Pumped-storage hydro is the only storage system that has had any appreciable application, and while some of these systems have storage as small as six hours, it is generally believed that ten to twelve hours is a safer specification.

In the case of dedicated storage, it is necessary to consider whether a reliability or availability problem is created by integrating the storage with a generating unit. This could result from the fact that when the generating unit is out of service for maintenance or because of a breakdown, the additional capacity of the storage discharge unit is also lost.

RENEWABLE ENERGY SOURCES

As an example of a renewable energy source, consider solar electric power, produced through a photovoltaic or thermodynamic process. A solar generating unit will have a rated output which is determined by the rating of the dc to ac inverter or of the steam turbine generator. The rated output will be achieved whenever the solar radiation, or insolation, equals or exceeds some selected design level, probably close to the nominal maximum of one kW per square meter (0.093 kW/sq. ft.) with insolation normal to the receiving surface. Depending on the type of collector and sun-tracking used, the unit output may remain near rated during most of the daylight hours if there is no atmospheric obscuration. When there is heavy cloud cover, the output is zero.

Since even short-term weather forecasting is not a precise science, it is understandable that the operator of a generation system might consider a solar unit to be unpredictable, and, hence, not useful in scheduling generation to meet daily loads. He would, however, accept the output of the unit whenever it was available because its incremental (and total) fuel cost is zero. Two aspects of the value of such a generating unit can thus be recognized: value as *capacity* to reliably meet a power demand; and value as a supplier of low-cost *energy*. The solar plant would appear to be poor at the former and good at the latter.

Capacity Value

But the capacity value of a solar unit is not zero, any more than that of a fossil-steam unit is 100%. Consider their comparative outage performances: the fossil-steam unit has predictable outages for scheduled maintenance of perhaps 15% of the time; the solar unit has predictable nighttime outages of about 50%, during which some maintenance can be accomplished, and another 5% or 10% for the balance of scheduled maintenance. Regarding forced outages: the fossil unit's rate may be from 5% to 15%; the solar unit's mechanical forced-outage rate may be in the same range, with an additional 10% to 30% unpredictable insolation outage. So it is not correct to say that the conventional unit is predictable and the solar unpredictable: they have differing degrees of unpredictability.

The capacity value of a solar unit, as well as of a conventional unit, is measured by its effective capacity, as defined in Chapter 9. Although the Garver approximation might be used for solar units, that would require the definition of a 'solar forced-outage rate.' A simpler method is to calculate the system

LOLP with and without the solar unit, and determine its effective capacity as the difference in system load-carrying capacity (see Fig. 9.1).

In order to do this, the LOLP calculation must be performed hourly rather than daily. The solar unit is not included in the outage table; instead, its actual hourly output is used to reduce the values of the load model (in effect, to serve the load), thus altering the hourly probabilities of insufficient capacity, and consequently, the total for the year. The LOLP is, of course, measured in hours per year instead of days per year when this procedure is used.

The hourly output of the solar unit must be obtained by appropriate calculations starting with hourly data on insolation and incorporating the performance characteristics of the particular kind of solar plant. The insolation data derive from historical records, and there is considerable variation from year to year. It is desirable, therefore, to calculate several years of data and use for evaluation purposes the year that gives the lowest value of effective capacity.

Studies of photovoltaic (EPRI, 1978b) and wind (EPRI, 1978c) power in electric utility systems have shown effective capacities as high as 65% for wind, and approaching 70% for solar. Values as low as 10% have also been noted. The wide variation in results is a function not only of the magnitude of the site-related solar or wind resource, but also of its timing relative to the daily load cycle. Solar or wind power plant output occurring at the time of a daily peak load is most effective in reducing system LOLP. For this reason, analyses of these power sources should include a maximum range of weather data, as well as consideration of possible future changes in load patterns. Given a reasonable penetration (no more than 5% to 10% of system capacity), it is believed that even a most conservative analysis will concede some capacity credit to solar or wind plants; i.e. in the long range, the system's installed conventional generating capacity may be reduced because of their presence. Their capacity value becomes the capital cost of the conventional capacity omitted.

Energy Value

In determining the energy value of these power plants, a conventional production-costing procedure is used (Fig. 11.5), with the plant output modifying the hourly loads, much as is done with hydro. Again, the analysis should consider a maximum range of weather data, perhaps selecting a long-term average historical year for final calculations.

The capacity factor of solar plants may approach 35% in areas of good insolation, while those of wind plants may be considerably higher, depending on wind regime and the wind speed at which a particular plant is designed to produce rated output. The economic value of the energy produced depends upon its timing relative to the operation of the conventional plants that would otherwise be required to operate, their heat rates, and fuel costs. The energy value of solar or wind plants may be expressed as the capitalized value of fuel saved over the lifetime of the plants.

To summarize, the analysis of renewable energy resources follows the procedure of total system analysis illustrated in Fig. 11.1, treating them as load modifiers on a long-term probabilistic basis. The sum of capacity and energy values is the capital investment in these plants which may be economically justified. Detailed descriptions of the value/cost analysis procedure are given in both EPRI (1978b) and EPRI (1978c).

Energy Storage and Renewable Sources

It is sometimes stated, as an axiom, that solar or wind power plants, to be useful, must incorporate some form of energy storage. This is true if one conceives of such plants as the sole, or major, power supply for some isolated load. Very large amounts of storage would be required to assure supplying the load during the days or weeks of unfavorable weather that might be anticipated. But such applications would be highly specialized ones that have nothing to do with electric utility generating systems, where the penetration of solar or wind power in the foreseeable future will likely be small.

The Electric Power Research Institute studies cited previously showed that dedicated storage tended to increase capacity value and decrease energy value, giving a small net increase in value. But the added capital cost was several times the added value, even using optimistic assumptions for the cost of advanced storage devices. On the other hand, it was shown that the same storage devices applied as general system storage could be justified economically in many cases.

We may conclude, then, that energy storage is not 'needed' in order to apply solar or wind generation to utility systems in moderate amounts; and that if storage is to be beneficial it will be general storage, free to be operated for total system economy.

14
Direct Unit Comparisons

Direct unit cost comparisons are those in which only the costs of the alternate units in question are calculated. Although the costs of other existing or future system units are excluded, their presence may be taken into account in the selection of the capacity factor to be used. There are two general situations in which direct unit cost comparisons are indicated. The first occurs after a total system analysis, when the type and approximate size of unit has been selected for the next addition to a generating system. It then becomes necessary to engage in a series of economic investigations, ranging from the selection of specific steam conditions and cycle configuration, in the case of steam units, to the choice of vendors for major plant components, to the design of auxiliary drive systems. All of these questions require balancing of capital cost and production cost, for which direct unit cost comparisons are generally adequate.

The criterion for adequacy in these situations is that the direct unit cost comparison should produce a close approximation to the impact of the alternate units or designs on total system cost. This means that the alternates, if installed on the generating system, could be expected to perform in the same economic and operational application mode (i.e. base load, midrange, or peaking), which in turn requires that unit sizes, fuel costs per kWh, and operational flexibilities be reasonably similar.

The second situation in which direct unit cost comparisons may be used occurs when the application modes of the alternates are known to be dissimilar, or are unknown. Here, the gross approximation method of 'screening curves' is used, not for decision-making, but for illustrating relationships or providing perspective.

Two detailed methods, Cost of Electricity and Lifecycle Costs are discussed, followed by a description of the screening curve method.

UNIT COST OF ELECTRICITY: $/MWh

The reader will recall that the costs associated with a generating unit are of two kinds: fixed and variable. The fixed costs consist of capital investment and certain items of operation and maintenance cost. Fixed costs are logically expressed in dollars per year (the capital cost being multiplied by the fixed-charge rate to obtain this result). Fixed costs exist whether the unit is operated or not.

Variable costs consist of fuel cost and certain other components of operation and maintenance cost. They are logically expressed in $/MWh because the costs are truly a linear function of generated energy.

Alternate proposed units have differing cost, both fixed and variable. To compare them requires some kind of total-cost criterion: either the fixed cost must be translated into variable terms and added to the real variable cost, or vice versa. It is a simple calculation—all that is needed is an assumed capacity factor.

Cost of Electricity (COE—sometimes called 'busbar cost') employs this device. It converts fixed costs to equivalent variable costs and expresses the total in $/MWh. The unit having the lowest total COE is the economic choice. This method is widely used—perhaps because it seems so simple; and perhaps for the same reason, it widely produces misleading results. The calculation is as follows:

$$\text{COE} = 10^3 \, [D \times (\text{fcr}) + O_f]/(8760 \times C_f) + O_v + h \times F \times 10^{-3}, \quad (14.1)$$

where COE = Cost of Electricity, $/MWh
D = plant cost, $/kW
fcr = level fixed-charge rate, p.u.
O_f = Fixed O&M cost, $/kW-yr
O_v = Variable O&M cost, $/MWh
C_f = Capacity factor, per unit
h = heat rate, kJ/kWh (Btu/kWh)
F = fuel price, $/GJ ($/MBtu).

The essence of the COE method is its unit of measurement, $/MWh; and this is the source of its potential error. Recall the discussions in Chapter 10 of similar ratios, kJ/kWh and $/kW, where it was noted how careful one must be that the numerators and denominators be measured on the same basis for all alternates. The same admonition applies to $/MWh, but in addition, there is the problem that the denominator, MWh, is not inherently a measure of the usefulness, value, or 'goodness' of a generating unit; so to normalize costs to unconditional MWh is meaningless. The following points will clarify this:

1. Although the plant costs, D, of alternate units may be consistently derived, the actual ratings may be different. If so, the alternates cannot deliver the same amount of energy to the system and cannot equally contribute to system

load-carrying capability, or reliability. But COE does not measure these fundamental differences.

2. Even at the same rating, alternate units cannot contribute equally to system reliability if their forced-outage rates are different. COE makes no provision for this.

3. It should be clear that the same value of C_f should be assumed for all alternates so that equal annual energies are compared . But this may be an impossible assumption to make if forced-outage rates are different. COE does not take this into account.

As has been stated, direct unit cost comparisons, to be rational, must approximate the effects of alternate units on total system cost. This requires the overt recognition that each generating unit contributes both capacity and energy to the system and that both must be equal before cost comparisons can be made. It is possible to recast and revise the COE method to accomplish this, but it is seldom done. Consequently, it is recommended that a completely different approach be used: calculate Lifecycle Cost, a methodology which incorporates a discipline to assure comparability of units.

LIFECYCLE COSTS: $/YEAR

In this method, each unit's cost is calculated in $/year for the same specified amount of capacity and energy contribution to the system. Changing operational and economic conditions during the units' lifetimes are specifically recognized and included in the evaluation wherever feasible.

Although it is always difficult to estimate these future conditions, it is impossible to avoid doing so if an evaluation is to be made. If one attempts to avoid uncertainty about the future by studying only ten years of the units' lives, this is equivalent to saying that the last twenty years will be identical to the first ten. Almost any assumption is usually better than this. So the evaluation should consider the total unit life; but this does not mean that twenty or thirty yearly calculations need be made. Since the time cost of money must be recognized in any case, advantage may be taken of the leveling methods discussed in Chapter 4, thus making a single year's calculation represent total life.

Capacity Cost

One of the alternate units is selected as a base unit for comparison. Its effective capacity is calculated using eqn (9.8), and designated L_0, the value to which all other alternates will be adjusted. The capacity cost of the base unit is

$$G_0 = C_0 [D_0 \times (\text{fcr}) + O_{f_0}], \qquad (14.2)$$

where G_0 = capacity cost, \$/yr

$\quad C_0$ = base-unit capacity, kW

$\quad D_0$ = base-unit plant cost, \$/kW

$\quad$ fcr = level fixed-charge rate, p.u.

$\quad O_{f_0}$ = fixed O&M cost, \$/kW-yr.

The capacity cost of alternate units is

$$G = C[D \times (\text{fcr}) + O_f] + (L_0 - L)S_c, \qquad (14.3)$$

where G = capacity cost, \$/yr

$\quad\quad C$ = alternate-unit capacity, kW

$\quad\quad D$ = alternate-unit plant cost, \$/kW

$\quad\quad O_f$ = alternate-unit fixed O&M cost, \$/kW-yr

$\quad L_0, L$ = effective capacities, base and alternate units, kW

$\quad\quad S_c$ = system replacement capacity cost, \$/kW-yr.

The term $(L_0 - L)S_c$ in eqn (14.3) compensates for differences in both rated capacity and forced-outage rate between base and alternate units. It is frequently convenient to take as the value of S_c the annual cost of firm capacity purchased (without energy) from neighboring systems; or it may be valued as the annual fixed charge on the effective capacity of peaking generation, such as gas turbines, which would not generate appreciable energy.

Energy Cost (Preliminary)

The Energy-cost calculations adjust each alternate unit's cost to the energy of the base unit selected above. A major consideration in this process is the selection of capacity factor. Since the procedure involves making a single-year calculation represent lifetime costs, the capacity factor used must be a level equivalent of actual anticipated future yearly values. Future trends of capacity factor are best estimated from production-cost simulations; past trends are also useful guides. In any case, it is assumed that future-capacity factors will be determined, basically, by economic dispatch, and that the fuel-cost characteristics of base and alternate units are similar enough so that capacity factors may be assumed equal. The one exception to this is the effect of forced outages, which, being random, will independently affect the ability of a unit to operate at a designated capacity factor.

The energy produced by the base unit is

$$W_0 = C_0 \times 8760 \times C_f, \qquad (14.4)$$

where W_0 = base energy, kWh/yr

$\quad\quad C_f$ = designated capacity factor, p.u.

It is assumed that the designated capacity factor is attained by the base unit considering its own forced-outage rate and that the capacity factor of alternate units will be higher or lower depending on their forced-outage rates. It is difficult, in a direct unit comparison, to assess the impact of variations in planned maintenance, or planned outage rate, on either energy production or effective capacity; hence such differences, even if known, are usually neglected. The energy of alternate units is:

$$W = C \times 8760 \times C_f(1 - R_f)/(1 - R_{f_0}), \tag{14.5}$$

where W = alternate-unit energy, kWh/yr
  R_f = forced-outage rate of alternate unit, p.u.
  R_{f_0} = forced-outage rate of base unit, p.u.

The energy cost of the base unit is:

$$E_0 = W_0(h_0 \times F_0/10^6 + O_{v_0}/10^3), \tag{14.6}$$

where E_0 = energy cost of base unit, \$/yr
  h_0 = heat rate, kJ/kWh (Btu/kWh)
  F_0 = fuel price, \$/GJ (\$/MBtu)
  O_{v_0} = variable O&M cost, \$/MWh

The energy cost of alternate units is:

$$E = W(h \times F/10^6 + O_v/10^3) + (W_0 - W)S_e/10^3, \tag{14.7}$$

where E = alternate-unit energy cost, \$/yr
  h = heat rate of alternate unit, kJ/kWh (Btu/kWh)
  F = fuel price of alternate unit, \$/GJ (\$/MBtu)
  O_v = variable O&M cost \$/MWh
  S_e = system replacement energy cost, \$/MWh.

The term $(W_0 - W)S_e$ normalizes the energy cost of the alternate units to the energy generated by the base unit, under the assumption that any deficiency must be made up by other system units at varying fuel and O&M costs during the life of the alternate unit. The value of S_e is constrained to be equal to or larger than the sum of fuel and variable O&M costs of the alternate unit because the principle of economic dispatch states that, when the alternate unit is operating, there can be no other *unloaded* system unit of lower cost operating. S_e is also subject to change with time because of inflation and the changing makeup of system generation.

The best estimate of S_e is obtained from the results of a production-cost simulation. Alternatively, S_e may be taken as the average fuel and O&M costs of system units whose costs are greater than those of the alternate unit, recognizing any change with time, as noted above. It is also well to recognize that for much of the time, the energy will be supplied at the incremental, not total, cost of fuel and O&M. S_e must, of course, be a level value.

Equations (14.6) and (14.7) must be considered preliminary, pending a consideration of levelized values.

Calculating Level Values

The general expression for the equivalent level value of a nonuniform series is:

$$R = (CRF)_{n,r} \sum_1^n \frac{R(y)}{(1 + r)^y}. \qquad (14.8)$$

This equation may be used to develop level values of S_c, O_f, C_f, F, O_v, and S_e for use in the capacity and energy cost expressions given above. In many cases, however, it is possible to represent the future trends of these quantities as linear or exponential equations, and this greatly simplifies the procedure, as the following paragraphs illustrate.

Leveling the Capacity Factor. The curve of Fig. 14.1 is one estimate of how the capacity factor of a unit might vary over its life, from 0.8 for years 1 to 5 and declining thereafter with a gradient of 0.03/yr., ending at 0.05. The present worth of this series may be calculated as the difference between the present worth (P_1) of a uniform series of 0.8 for 30 years and that (P_2) of a gradient, or arithmetic, series increasing from 0 in year 5 to 0.75 in year 30. See eqn (4.17).

$$P_1 - P_2 = \frac{0.8}{(CRF)_{30}} - \frac{1}{(1 + r)^4}\left[\frac{0.03}{r}\left(\frac{1}{(CRF)_{26}} - \frac{26}{(1 + r)^{26}}\right)\right]. \qquad (14.9)$$

For $r = 0.12$,

$$P_1 - P_2 = 5.40665.$$

The level value of the capacity factor, $\bar{C}_f$, is the present worth times $(CRF)_{30}$, or

$$\bar{C}_f = 5.40665 \times 0.12414 = 0.671. \qquad (14.10)$$

Leveling the Fuel and O&M Costs. The estimate of the trend of future fuel (or O&M) costs can be expressed in any form, but a common and convenient assumption is that it will be exponential:

$$F(y) = F(1)(1 + u)^{y-1}, \qquad (14.11)$$

where $F(y)$ = fuel cost, year y
u = inflation rate, per unit.

The level equivalent of such a series may be obtained by use of eqn (4.14):

$$\bar{F} = F(1)(CRF)_{n,r}\left[1 - \left(\frac{1 + u}{1 + r}\right)^n\right]/(r - u), \qquad (14.12)$$

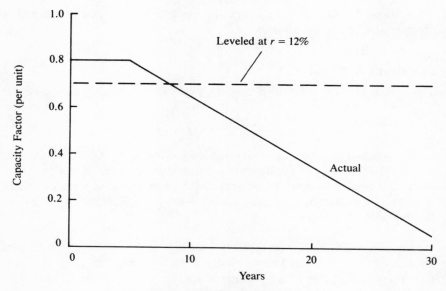

Fig. 14.1. Capacity factor trend.

where $\bar{F}$ = level fuel cost

$F(1)$ = fuel cost in first year of unit operation

r = discount rate

n = unit life, years.

If the yearly change in fuel cost is expected to be linear rather than exponential, a similar factor may be obtained using eqn (4.18). Failing this, the general equation may be used:

$$\bar{F} = (\text{CRF})_{n,r} \sum_{1}^{n} F(y)/(1 + r)^y. \qquad (14.13)$$

Similar procedures are employed to obtain level values of the O&M costs, O_v and O_f.

Figure 14.2 shows a fuel-cost inflation curve of the form of eqn (14.11), where $F(1) = 1.0$, and $u = 0.08$. The equivalent level value is shown, calculated from eqn (14.12), taking $r = 0.12$ and $n = 30$:

$$\bar{F} = 1.0 \times 0.12414 \times 16.603 = 2.061. \qquad (14.14)$$

Leveling the Product. If eqns (14.4) and (14.5) are substituted in eqn (14.7), giving the detailed expression for energy cost, it will be noted that the only time-variant elements of the equation are C_f, F, O_v, and S_e. Further, the last three each appear as a product with C_f. Since these are all usually leveled elements, it is necessary to consider the error inherent in products of level values. Consider the capacity-factor and fuel-cost curves of Figs. 14.1 and 14.2. If, instead of using level values for a 'single year' calculation, the total energy

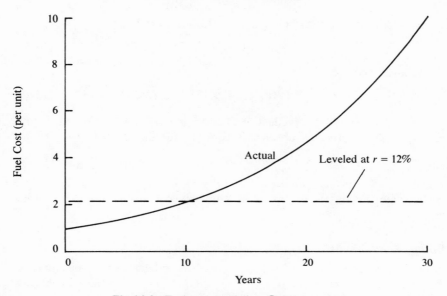

Fig.14.2. Fuel-cost escalation @ 8% per year.

cost were calculated for each year, then leveled, the early years would see a high capacity factor paired with a low fuel price, and the later years the opposite. This is not the same as the product of $\bar{C}_f$ and $\bar{F}$. Mathematically, $\overline{C_f \times F} \neq \bar{C}_f \times \bar{F}$, or

$$(CRF)_{n,r} \sum_{1}^{n} \frac{C_f(y) \times F(y)}{(1 + r)^y} \neq (CRF)_{n,r} \left[\sum_{1}^{n} \frac{C_f(y)}{(1 + r)^y} \right] \times \left[\sum_{1}^{n} \frac{F(y)}{(1 + r)^y} \right]. \quad (14.15)$$

The error may be appreciable, as an example will illustrate. In order to obtain the level value of the product of C_f and F, as given in Figs. 14.1 and 14.2, the series must be divided into two series: one for years 1 to 4; and the second for years 5 to 30.

Because the capacity factor is constant at $C_f = 0.8$ for years 1 to 4, the present worth for these years is simply the product of C_f and the present worth of an exponential series, given by eqn (4.14):

$$P_{1-4} = 0.8 \times 1.0[1 - \left(\frac{1.08}{1.12}\right)^4]/(0.12 - 0.08) = 2.708. \quad (14.16)$$

The present worth of the second series is given by eqn (4.19) as of year 5, where $F(5) = 1.0(1.08)^4 = 1.36$, $C_f(5) = 0.8$, $g = 0.03$, $k = 1.08/1.12 = 0.9643$, and $n = 26$.

$$P_{5-30} = 10.091 \text{ (as of year 5).} \quad (14.17)$$

The total present worth for years 1 to 30, as of year 1, is:

$$P_{1-30} = 2.708 + 10.091/(1.12)^4 = 9.121. \tag{14.18}$$

The level value is:

$$\overline{C_f \times F} = P_{1-30} \times CRF_{30,0.12} = 9.121 \times 0.12414 = 1.132. \tag{14.19}$$

This is the correct level product of C_f and F over the 30-year period; but the product of the level values obtained in eqns (14.10) and (14.14) is:

$$\bar{C}_f \times \bar{F} = 0.671 \times 2.061 = 1.383, \tag{14.20}$$

which is 22% too high, meaning that calculated energy costs are 22% high. Under some circumstances, this could throw the economic choice to the wrong unit.

Energy Cost (Final)

In order to recognize the importance of levelized products of the quantities in the energy-cost calculation, eqns (14.6) and (14.7) are combined with eqns (14.4) and (14.5) and rearranged as follows:

$$E_0 = 8760 \times C_0 (h_0 \times \overline{C_f \times F}/10^6 + \overline{C_f \times O_{v_0}} /10^3). \tag{14.21}$$

$$E = 8760 \times C[(1 - R_f)/(1 - R_{f_0})][h \times \overline{C_f \times F}/10^6 + \overline{C_f \times O_v}/10^3] \\ + 8760[C - C_0(1 - R_f)/(1 - R_{f_0})] \overline{C_f \times S_e}/10^3. \tag{14.22}$$

In these equations, $\overline{C_f \times F}$, etc., represent the level equivalents of the products of the two quantities; other symbols are as defined for eqns (14.4) through (14.7).

Example of Lifecycle Cost

As. an example of the Lifecycle Cost calculation, consider Table 14.1, which gives data for a base and alternate unit, and data common to both. In the following calculations, the values for C and C_0 will be expressed in millions of kW (GW) so as to produce results in millions of $. From eqn (9.8) the effective capacities are calculated to be:

$$L_0 = 0.4266 \, GW; \tag{14.23}$$

$$L = 0.4053 \, GW. \tag{14.24}$$

The capacity costs are calculated using eqns (14.2) and (14.3):

$$G_0 = 0.5(950 \times 0.18 + 4) = 87.5 \, M\$, \tag{14.25}$$

and

$$G = 0.49(930 \times 0.18 + 4) + (0.4266 - 0.4053) \times 50 = 85.1 \, M\$. \tag{14.26}$$

Assuming the capacity factor trend to be as shown in Fig. 14.1 and the

Table 14.1. Data for lifecycle cost calculation.

	Base Unit		Alternate Unit
Capacity, C, MW	500		490
Plant Cost, D, $/kW	950		930
Heat Rate, h, kJ/kWh	9 500		10 000
(Btu/kWh)	(9 005)		(9 479)
Fuel Price, F, $/GJ	1.65		1.65
($/MBtu)	(1.74)		(1.74)
O&M Cost, O_{f}, $/kW-yr	4.0		4.0
O&M Cost, O_v, $/MWh	2.4		2.5
Forced-Outage Rate, R_f, p.u.	0.10		0.12
Discount Rate, r, p.u.		0.12	
Inflation Rate, u, p.u.		0.08	
fcr, p.u.		0.18	
Life, n, yr.		30	
LOLP slope, M, MW		600	
System replacement capacity cost, S_c, $/kW-yr		50	
System replacement energy cost, S_e, $/MWh		22.0	

escalation of fuel, O&M, and system replacement energy cost all to be at the 8% rate of Fig. 14.2, the level capacity factor products may be obtained using the factor developed in eqn (14.19):

$$\overline{C_f \times F_0} = \overline{C_f \times F} = 1.132 \times 1.65 = 1.87; \qquad (14.27)$$

$$\overline{C_f \times O_{v_0}} = 1.132 \times 2.4 = 2.72; \qquad (14.28)$$

$$\overline{C_f \times O_v} = 1.132 \times 2.5 = 2.83; \qquad (14.29)$$

$$\overline{C_f \times S_e} = 1.132 \times 22 = 24.9. \qquad (14.30)$$

The unit energy cost may now be calculated using eqns (14.21) and (14.22):

$$E_0 = 8760 \times 0.500(9500 \times 1.87/10^6 + 2.72/10^3) = 89.7 \text{ M\$/yr.} \qquad (14.31)$$

$$E = 8760 \times 0.49[(0.88/0.9)(10\,000 \times 1.87/10^6 + 2.83/10^3] \\ + 8760[0.5 - 0.49(0.88/0.9)]24.9/10^3 = 94.9 \text{ M\$/yr.} \qquad (14.32)$$

The total lifecycle costs (LC) are:

$$LC_0 = 87.5 + 89.7 = 177.2 \text{ M\$/yr;} \qquad (14.33)$$

$$LC = 85.1 + 94.9 = 180.0 \text{ M\$/yr.} \qquad (14.34)$$

Because these are 30-year level values, the present worth of each may be obtained directly by use of the $(\text{CRF})_{30,0.12}$:

$$P_o = 177.2/0.12414 = 1427 \text{ M\$;} \qquad (14.35)$$

$$P = 180.0/0.12414 = 1450 \text{ M\$.} \qquad (14.36)$$

It would be possible to transmute either the annual level or present-worth values into $/MWh by dividing by some equivalent-level annual value of kWh, or a 'present worth' kWh value; but since the divisor would logically have to be the same for the base unit and the alternate unit, no additional intelligence would be gained, and not even any new perspective, since the magnitudes would be so much greater than the $/MWh costs of current units to which one might be mentally calibrated.

There is one perspective which can be valuable because it is a current cost: capital cost. The difference in annual costs may be converted to an equivalent capital cost difference.

$$\Delta \text{ Capital Cost} = (LC - LC_0)/\text{fcr}. \tag{14.37}$$

Using the results of this example,

$$\Delta \text{ Capital Cost} = (180.0 - 177.2)/0.18 = 15.6 \text{ M\$}. \tag{14.38}$$

This result states that the total plant (capital) cost of the alternate unit would have to be reduced by 15.6 M$ to secure a break-even with the base unit. This amounts to 31.8 $/kW on its own rating base.

SCREENING CURVES

The screening curve is simply a plot of unit annual cost as a function of capacity factor. It is not a direct unit evaluation method in the sense that it could be thought of as an alternative to lifecycle cost calculations. Recall that the latter is for use in comparing units whose operational and application modes are the same. Care is taken to adjust for small differences in unit size and forced-outage rate and to recognize future changes in capacity factor. The attempt is made to have the differences in unit costs closely approximate the differences in total system cost which would obtain were the units to be alternatively installed in a total system cost analysis.

Screening curves, on the other hand, are most frequently useful for gross comparisons of units of *different* economic application modes—or, perhaps, to discover, or illustrate, what those modes would be for new or unfamiliar types of generation.

Screening Curve Equations

Capacity cost in $/yr is given by eqns (14.2) and (14.3). Since the screening curve does not distinguish among sizes of units, it cannot recognize reliability effects, and eqn (14.3) is therefore inappropriate. Omitting the subscript, 0, and dividing eqn (14.2) by the rated capacity, C, gives,

$$G/C = D \times \text{fcr} + O_f, \tag{14.39}$$

where: G/C = capacity cost, $/kW-yr. Similarly, the energy cost eqn (14.21)

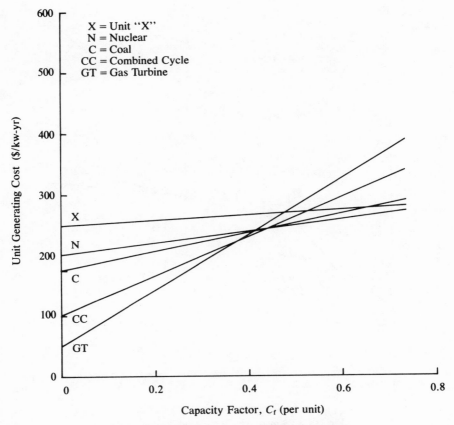

Fig. 14.3. Screening curves (without escalation).

becomes,

$$E/C = 8760 \times C_f(h \times F/10^6 + O_v/10^3), \qquad (14.40)$$

where E/C = energy cost, \$/kW-yr.

There is no need to consider the level products of C_f because in this equation C_f is an unspecified variable.

The screening 'curve' of each unit is a plot of $G/C + E/C$ vs. C_f. It is, of course, a straight line with intercept = G/C and slope = $8760(h \times F/10^6 + O_v/10^3)$.

Interpretation of Screening Curves

Figure 14.3 is a typical set of screening curves using the data of Table 12.3 for the nuclear, combined-cycle, and gas turbine units. The coal unit is the base unit of Table 14.1. Unit X is a hypothetical unit having higher capital cost but

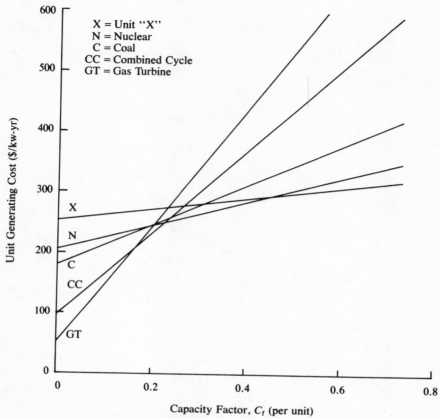

Fig. 14.4. Screening curves (with escalation).

lower fuel cost than the nuclear unit. No escalation of fuel or O&M costs is included in Fig. 14.3.

Inspection of Fig. 14.3 leads to the observation that for base-load application ($C_f > 0.5$) the nuclear unit appears best; and that for peaking ($C_f < 0.35$) the gas turbine has lowest cost. In a small capacity factor range around 0.4, the combined-cycle seems viable, but the coal unit is a close contender. Unit X has been 'screened out' of contention because it does not have lowest cost at any capacity factor.

This is about all that can be said. There is no basis for concluding that one or another of the units should be selected for the next addition to a system, because nothing is known about the economic characteristics of the existing generation. If, as an extreme example, it consisted entirely of nuclear units, it is certain that a total system cost study would direct the immediate addition of peaking units; and, of course, the opposite extreme would dictate nuclear unit additions. One might suspect that the general application of combined-cycle and coal units would be more restricted than the other two, either as to the number of susceptible utility systems or the penetration into any one system; but this would not be a very firm conclusion.

The complexion of screening curves changes markedly with changes in assumptions, owing to the small angles between the curves. Figure 14.4 gives a set of curves developed from the same data as Figure 14.3, but assuming 8% per year escalation of fuel and O&M costs. The leveling factor, 2.061, developed in eqn (14.14), was applied to the quantities O_f, F, and O_v in eqns (14.39) and (14.40). Now the balance of fuel and capital costs has shifted to favor the lower-fuel-cost unit X, which takes over the highest capacity factor range, leaving the nuclear unit to a midrange application. There is still a narrow range for the combined-cycle unit, but the coal unit seems now to be definitely out of the running. The gas turbine remains secure in its peaking role, but with much reduced capacity factor range.

SUMMARY

Direct unit cost comparisons are useful to select among closely competing units of the same type after desired unit size and heat rate have been decided by total system cost studies; and to discover or illustrate competitive economic application ranges of dissimilar units. For the latter purpose, screening curves are simple, direct, and sufficiently accurate. For the former purpose, the Cost of Electricity ($/MWh) method, although widely used, is ambiguous and error-prone. Lifecycle Cost comparisons are more time-consuming to perform, but they inherently promote understanding, completeness, and accuracy, and are much to be preferred.

15
Summary
and Future Development

It has been shown in the preceding chapters that the *purpose* of generation economic studies is to provide the economic basis for management decision with respect to capital investment in generating facilities. There are always other bases for decision—political, societal, environmental, and strategic—whose urgencies may at times loom so large as to make economic considerations seem almost trivial by comparison. But utility management—and electricity consumers as well—must, if nothing else, know the price to be paid for concessions to noneconomic constraints. And in most instances, the existence of such constraints still leaves room for economic decisions—to select, as it were, the *least uneconomic* alternative.

The *criterion of economic choice* is least cost to the consumer, which translates into minimum revenue requirements for the utility. This is fundamental, whether the utility is investor-owned and regulated by a government commission or government-sponsored and operating directly for the benefit of consumers. The fact that a fair rate of return on investment is 'allowed' does not mean that imprudent investments are permissible; and the existence, for example, of automatic fuel 'pass-through' provisions does not ultimately relieve utility management of the responsibility to make decisions that will produce electricity at the minimum cost.

The *method* of generation economics is *simulation*—on two levels. First is the simulation of the utility system of accounts, which, through the mechanisms of fixed-charge rate and time value of money, produces cost to the consumer. Beneath this is the simulation of system operation, which, under the constraints of the system load, the need to serve it reliably, and the capabilities of individual generating units, develops the production costs necessary to obtain total revenue requirements. There are degrees of approximation in this process, from the total system analysis to direct unit comparisons, to screening curves.

While the methods of generation economic analysis seem highly developed, there will, no doubt, be further progress in providing management with the best possible economic decision information. Two of the areas of current concern and opportunity will be briefly discussed here.

ENVIRONMENTAL CONTROLS

The potential impacts of electric utility generating plants on the quality of the environment may be classed as esthetic and as those of air and water pollution. The first arises when a plant is perceived as visually unattractive—a 'blot on the landscape'—or when its operation tends to reduce the beauty or spectacle of a natural resource. An example of the latter is the hydroelectric plants located at Niagara Falls, New York, whose operation is curtailed during the tourist season so as to maintain an impressive flow in the cataract.

Air pollution is of growing concern in many parts of the world, and although electric utility power plants are not the major offenders, controls are being applied to their discharges into the atmosphere. Particulates and the oxides of nitrogen and sulfur are of most importance.

Water pollution resulting from the need for condenser cooling in steam power plants—sometimes termed 'thermal pollution'—can, in some circumstances, change the original biological equilibrium of a body of water used for cooling. The effects vary widely; and in some cases they are deleterious to marine life or to the character of the water as a recreational resource. In other cases, higher water temperatures may cause increases in the propagation of some forms of fish life. This effect may be applauded by fishing interests, but opposed by other groups as 'interfering with nature.'

Effects of Environmental Controls

The first obvious effect of environmental restrictions on generation economics is to increase the capital costs of plants. Consideration of esthetics and of air and water pollution may require remote siting of plants, with consequent increases in construction costs and transmission costs. Flue-gas desulfurizers, precipitators, and special combustion-system designs for control of air emissions all increase capital costs directly. If direct use of lake, river, and ocean water for condenser cooling is prohibited, cooling towers and an alternate source of makeup water add to the plant cost. Taken together, environmental control of steam electric power plants may affect capital costs as much as 25%.

A second effect of environmental control is reduced efficiency. Net station heat rate may be increased 5% or more as the result of the larger auxiliary-power requirements of anti-pollution equipment and the degradation of thermodynamic efficiency from higher cooling-water temperature, hence increased back-pressure.

A third potential cost effect exists in some extremely critical areas of air-quality control where, at times, it may be necessary to dispatch units not on the basis of incremental cost, but to minimize air emissions.

Most of these environmental-control effects on generation economic studies may be recognized as constraints, and implemented by adjustment of the plant cost and efficiency inputs to the study. The overall result will be to favor those plant types and fuel types least subject to environmental cost, and, as noted in Chapter 12, possibly to force smaller unit and plant sizes.

The methodology of generation studies may require modification in two ways, and, as always, the watchword is simulation of both financial and technical operations. On the one hand, government may provide tax incentives or loan guarantees for anti-pollution equipment, which will require calculation of a separate fixed-charge rate for the proportion of plant investment so represented. On the other, the production-cost simulation will require modification for those few cases, mentioned above, where noneconomic dispatch is used to control area air quality.

UNCERTAINTY

Uncertainty has plagued mankind at least since the first caveman wondered whether he should risk the ire of the saber-toothed tiger by invading his hunting grounds. Utilities, like every other kind of business enterprise, have always had to deal with uncertainty; indeed, it is the basis of the free enterprise concept of risk capital investment. But whether today's climate of inflation, potential fuel shortages, and environmental constraints represents an area of uncertainty greater than in the past is unimportant: wherever progress can be made to reduce the negative impacts of uncertainty, it should be made.

There are two areas of uncertainty that are routinely included in generation economic studies. The uncertainty of the availability of generating units is recognized by providing reserve capacity based on probability mathematics. This same uncertainty may be incorporated in production-cost simulations to give not an absolute, but a probabilistic, cost of fuel, operation, and maintenance. But in both of these instances, loads are represented deterministically. Load forecast uncertainty may be incorporated in LOLP calculations, but determining the economic effects of load-growth uncertainty requires different techniques.

Uncertainty of Load Growth

Alternate schedules of future load growth encompassing a reasonable range of values may be analyzed deterministically to establish required future capacity additions for each. The higher-load-growth scenarios will, of course, require more capacity, and vice versa. One way of testing the economic implications of load-growth uncertainty is to assume a capacity decision based on the higher load growth, then test it against the actual occurrence of the lower rate of growth by calculating total system costs over the forecast period. This would represent the case where the system capacity has turned out to be *overbuilt* relative to the load. The opposite situation, where the actuality is assumed to result in *under-building*, also would be analyzed for total system costs.

In the *overcapacity* case, capital costs are, of course, higher than necessary; but because of the high reserve margin, it is possible to avoid operating the peaking generation and the older units of high production cost, with the result that system production costs *per kWh* are very much lower than they would have been had the load more nearly matched the generation. The reverse situation applies to the *undercapacity* case, with the added possibility of the need to purchase high-cost emergency power when owned capacity is insufficient. Thus, excess cost of capacity may be overcome by savings in production cost, and vice versa.

A study performed for the Electric Power Research Institute (EPRI, 1979) suggests that in this situation, there may be an optimal choice of risking overbuilding rather than underbuilding. Another study (EPRI, 1978a) more explicitly examines uncertainty in load growth with similar conclusions. A study by Dees, Felak, and Jordan (1978) considers not only revenue requirements, but, using financial simulation, the impacts on electricity rates and earnings per share. These kinds of studies do not eliminate uncertainty of load growth, but may sharply reduce uncertainty as to the correct capacity *decision,* regardless of load growth.

Other Uncertain Parameters

It is fortunate when, as in the case of load uncertainty, countervailing forces seem to tend toward a narrow decision range over a wide range of uncertainty regarding some one parameter. Work is just beginning on the task of analyzing uncertainty in other parameters, notably costs of capital, labor, and fuel, and the rate of inflation. In principle, it should be possible to develop computer models in which cost inputs and even physical inputs, such as loads and unit forced-outage rates, are all expressed as probability distributions, with cost outputs similarly expressed. There are many facets to such an approach, such as correlation among parameters, that will be difficult to solve within the limits of acceptable computer running time and cost. It would appear, too, that much research will be necessary to develop the data basis of probability distributions of the inputs and the rationale for appraising the outputs.

In the meantime, much can be learned about the impacts of uncertainty by parametric studies in which inputs are varied one at a time to test the response of total system cost. While such an approach may not be as satisfying, technically, as an automatic modeling method, it still can provide management with important insight for the decision process.

Glossary

Ad valorem. Literally, 'according to the value.' Used to describe taxes quoted as a percentage of the value of a plant.

Capital stock. The amount of equity capital supplied by shareholders.

Commitment. The starting and synchronizing of a unit preparatory to loading.

Dispatch. The specification of the load to be assumed by a specific generating unit at a specific time.

Equity capital. Venture, or risk, capital; the ownership portion of total capitalization.

Escalation. The total price change over a period of time, measured in current dollars and expressed in percent per year; inflation.

Funds. Money, cash.

Heating value. The heat content of a fuel; the calorific value.

Higher Heating Value (HHV). The gross quantity of heat obtained from combustion of a fossil fuel, per unit of weight or volume.

Inflation. See *Escalation*.

Instability. An operating condition of a power system wherein one or more generators lose or approach losing synchronism with the remainder of the generators; characterized by wide swings of voltage and current and ultimate need to disconnect generators from the power system.

Interconnection. A group of utility systems, interconnected by transmission, taken as a whole.

Inventory. The stock of materials, supplies, or commodities kept on hand for use in operations.

Lower Heating Value (LHV). The net quantity of heat obtained from combustion of a fossil fuel, per unit of weight or volume.

Merit order. In order of fuel cost of generation.

Mill. One one-thousandth of a dollar.

Pass-through. A regulatory device by which fuel-price changes are automatically reflected in electricity rates.

Peak. The maximum actual or expected load for some period of time.

Per unit. The fraction of a whole denominated as unity; numerically equal to percent divided by 100.

Plant. (1) In accounting, the asset account in which is accumulated the investment in production facilities. (2) A generating facility at a single site consisting of one or more generating units.

Power pool. An interconnection characterized by joint operation, coordinated planning, and contractual agreements for interchange of energy and power.

Priority order. The sequence in which generating units will be committed in response to increasing load; usually the same as *merit order*.

Production cost. The total cost of generation, including fuel, operating labor, and maintenance labor and materials.

Rates. The prices paid for electricity, usually measured in $/MWh and/or $/kW.

Rating. The stated output of a generating unit under specified conditions of operation.

Regulation. The process by which a government agency sets the rates to be charged for electricity.

Saturation. The degree to which a product has achieved the maximum possible penetration of the market, e.g. 'refrigerators have reached 90% (of) saturation.'

Stack. Chimney.

System. The utility system, consisting of generation, transmission, and distribution components; the generation component.

Unit. A self-contained generating facility consisting of one or more prime-movers and generators having common auxiliaries and single control of output.

Working capital. Short-term investment necessary to current operation of an enterprise, e.g. materials, supplies, accounts receivable.

References

Abdelsamad, Moustafa H. (1973). *A Guide to Capital Expenditure Analysis*. AMACOM, a division of American Management Associations, New York.

AIEE Committee Report (1961). Application of probability methods to generation capacity problems. *AIEE Transactions on Power Apparatus and Systems*, Feb. 1961.

Albrecht, P. F., Marsh, W. D., and Kindl, F. H. (1970). Gas turbines require different outage criteria. *Electrical World*, April 27, 1970, pp. 38–40.

Allan, R. N., and Takieddien, F. N. (1977). Generation modeling in power system reliability evaluation. *IEE International Conference on Reliability of Power Supply Systems*, London, Feb. 21–23, 1977.

Baleriaux, H., Jamoulle, E., and de Guertechin, Linard (1967). Simulation de l'exploitation d'un parc de machines thermiques de production d'electricite couple a des stations de pomage. *Revue E (edition S.R.B.E.)*, Vol. V, No. 7, pp. 3–24.

Bary, C. W., and Brown, W.T. (1957). Some new mathematical aspects to fixed charges. *AIEE Transactions*, Pt. III (*Power Apparatus and Systems*), June 1957, p. 230.

Billinton, Roy (1971). Bibliography on the application of probability methods in power system reliability evaluation. *IEEE Transactions on Power Apparatus and Systems*, pp. 649–660.

———, Ringlee, R. J., and Wood, A. J. (1973). *Power System Reliability Calculations*. The M.I.T. Press, Cambridge, Mass.

Calabrese, G. (1947). Generating reserve capacity determined by the probability method. *AIEE Transactions*, Vol. 66, pp. 1439–1450.

Carlin, J. F., Lyons, R. H., Mitiguay, J. R., Murphy, E. F., Galloway, C. D., Sager, M. A., and Wood, A. J. (1969). Corporate model of an electric utility. *IEEE Spectrum*, June 1969, pp. 75–84.

Day, J. T., Federowicz, A. J., and Menge, E. E. (1973). Optimizing generation planning. *Power Engineering*, July 1973.

Dees, D. L., Felak, R. P., and Jordan, G. A. (1978). The effect of load growth uncertainty on generation system expansion planning. *Proceedings of the American Power Conference*, Vol. 40.

Drake, J. H., Mayall, R. B., Kirchmayer, L. K., and Wood, H. (1962). Optimum operation of a hydrothermal system. *AIEE Transactions*, Vol. 81, Pt. III, pp. 242–250.

EEI (1977). *Report on Equipment Availability for the Ten-Year Period, 1967–1976*. Publication No. 77-64, Edison Electric Institute, New York.

EPRI (1978a). *Costs and Benefits of Over/Under Capacity in Electric Power System Planning*. Electric Power Research Institute, Palo Alto, Calif., EA-927.

——— (1978b). *Requirements Assessment of Photovoltaic Power Plants in Electric Utility Systems*. Electric Power Research Institute, Palo Alto, Calif., ER-685.

——— (1978c). *Requirements Assessment of Wind Power Plants in Electric Utility Systems*. Electric Power Research Institute, Palo Alto, Calif., ER-978.

——— (1979). *Generation System Reliability Analysis for Future Cost/Benefit Studies*. Electric Power Research Institute, Palo Alto, Calif., EA-958.

Ewart, D. N., Dawes, M. H., Schulz, R. P., and Brower, A. S. (1978). Power response requirements for electric utility generating units. *Proceedings of the American Power Conference*, Vol. 40, pp. 1139–50.

Galloway, C. D., Kirchmayer, L. K., Marsh, W. D., and Mellor, A. G. (1960). An approach to peak load economics. *AIEE Transactions*, Pt. III, Vol. 79, pp. 527–535.

———, Landes, I. H., and Marsh, W. D. (1964). The role of pumped storage in generation systems. *Proceedings of the American Power Conference*, Vol. 26.

———, Marsh, W. D., and Miller, K. F. (1969). An investigation of long range trends in system generation composition. Joint ASME-IEEE Power Generation Conference, Sept. 21–25, 1969, Charlotte, N.C.

Garver, L. L. (1966). Effective load-carrying capability of generating units. *IEEE Transactions on Power Apparatus and Systems*, pp. 910–919.

——— (1972). Adjusting maintenance schedules to levelize risk. *IEEE Transactions*, PAS, Vol. 91, pp. 2057–2063.

——— (1978). The electric utilities. In *Handbook of Operations Research, Models, and Applications*, (ed. by Joseph J. Moder and Salah E. Elmaghraby), pp. 535–578. Van Nostrand Reinhold Co., New York.

Gordon, Myron J., and Shillinglaw, Gordon (1969). *Accounting: A Management Approach* (4th ed.). Richard D. Irwin, Inc., Homewood, Ill.

Heck, F. M., Jr. (1961). The cost of capital in economic studies. *AIEE Transactions Pt. III (Power Apparatus and Systems)*, Dec. 1961, p. 775.

Heukensfeldt Jansen, H. P. J. (1977). *Project Evaluation and Discounted Cash Flow*. North Holland Publishing Co., Amsterdam.

IEEE Task Group Report (1971). A four state model for estimation of outage risk for units in peaking service. *IEEE Transactions on Power Apparatus and Systems*, pp. 618–627.

Jenkins, R. T. and Joy, D. S. (1974). Wien automatic system planning package (WASP)— An electric utility optimal generation expansion planning computer code. Oak Ridge National Laboratory, ORNL-4945.

Jeynes, Paul H. (1968). *Profitability and Economic Choice*. Iowa State University Press, Ames.

Jordan, G. A., Marsh, W. D., Moisan, R. W., and Oplinger, J. L. (1976). The impact of load factor on economic generation patterns. *Proceedings of the American Power Conference*, Vol. 38, pp. 1147–1154.

Kirchmayer, L. K. (1958). *Economic Operation of Power Systems*, John Wiley & Sons, New York.

——, Mellor, A. G., O'Mara, J. F., and Stevenson, J. R. (1955). An investigation of the economic size of steam-electric generating units. *AIEE Transactions*, Pt. III, Vol. 74, pp. 600–614.

——, Mellor, A. G., and Simmons, H. O., Jr. (1957). The effect of interconnections on economic generation expansion patterns. *AIEE Transactions, Power Apparatus and Systems*, June 1957, pp. 203–214.

Marsh, W. D., and McClure, J. B. (1964). Combining fossil fueled high efficiency, nuclear fueled, pumped hydro, and peaking gas turbine plants for lower total generation costs. *Transactions of World Power Conference*, Lausanne Sectional Meeting, Sept. 13-17, 1964, Vol. I, p. 312.

——, Moisan, R. W., and Murrell, T. C. (1974). Perspectives on the design and application of generation planning programs. ORNL TM-4443 (Rev. 1), Collection of papers presented at the Nuclear Utilities Planning Methods Symposium, Chattanooga, Tenn., Jan. 16–18, 1974.

Peters, Robert A. (1974). *ROI: Practical Theory and Innovative Applications*. AMACOM, a division of American Management Associations, New York.

Tice, J. B. (1967). Performance Requirements for Generation Reserve (unpublished). General Electric Co., Electric Utility Systems Engineering Dept., Schenectady, N.Y.

Index